Trust Accounting in One Hour for Lawyers

Sheila M. Blackford

ABA LAW PRACTICE DIVISION
The Business of Practicing Law

Cover by Lachina

Printed in the United States of America.

21 20 19 18 17 5 4 3 2 1

Library of Congress Cataloging-in-Publication Data

Names: Blackford, Sheila M., author. | American Bar Association. Section of Law Practice Management, sponsoring body.
Title: Trust accounting in one hour for lawyers / Sheila Blackford.
Description: Chicago : American Bar Association, 2016.
Identifiers: LCCN 2016052315 (print) | LCCN 2016052658 (ebook) | ISBN 9781634257398 (print) | ISBN 9781634257404 (epub)
Subjects: LCSH: Attorney and client—Economic aspects—United States. | Trusts and trustees—United States. | IOLTA programs—United States.
Classification: LCC KF311 .B54 2016 (print) | LCC KF311 (ebook) | DDC 657/.47—dc23
LC record available at https://lccn.loc.gov/2016052315

Discounts are available for books ordered in bulk. Special consideration is given to state bars, CLE programs, and other bar-related organizations. Inquire at ABA Publishing, American Bar Association, 321 North Clark Street, Chicago, Illinois 60654-7598.

www.ShopABA.org

Table of Contents

APPENDICES

About the Author

Sheila M. Blackford
Oregon State Bar Professional Liability Fund, Tigard, Oregon

Sheila Blackford received her B.A. from Mills College and J.D. with Tax Law Concentration from McGeorge School of Law. A member of the Oregon State Bar since 2000, she is active with the American Bar Association Law Practice Division, where she was the Editor-in-Chief of *Law Practice* Magazine and Chair of the *Law Practice* Magazine Editorial Board (2011–2013), stepping down to battle breast cancer successfully. She was a member of the Section Council (2010–2016). She is a member of ABA Women Rainmakers, Center for Professional Responsibility, Client Development and Marketing Forum, Ethics and Professionalism Group, Law Firm Management Interest Group, Publishing Board, and Senior Lawyers Division. She is a Fellow of the American Bar Association Law Foundation and has been active with the ABA MCLE Review Project, serving as a co-chair of one of its working group committees.

Ms. Blackford has been an attorney practice management advisor for the Oregon State Bar Professional Liability Fund since 2005. She was a member of the adjunct faculty for University of Oregon School of Law, teaching law practice management (2010–2013). A former sole practitioner, she provides confidential practice management assistance to Oregon attorneys to reduce their risk of malpractice claims and ethics complaints. In addition to her legal experience, she has over ten years of teaching, marketing, and advertising experience.

She has been a frequent speaker about practice management for law-related organizations. She is the co-author with Donna Neff of the ABA Law Practice Division book *Paperless in One Hour for Lawyers* (2014) and a chapter author in the ABA Law Practice Division book *Flying Solo: A Survival Guide for the Solo and Small Firm Lawyer,* 5th Edition (2014), and in the Oregon State Bar book *Fee Agreement Compendium* (2007). In between writing articles and CLE materials, she writes the *Just Oregon Lawyers* blog, and feeds her Twitter account, which brought her recognition as *One of the 50 Lawyers to Follow on Twitter* from Legal Productivity (2015).

Acknowledgments

I dedicate this writing effort to my husband Eric Blackford and my daughter Michele LaMerrill and son-in-law Martyn Smith who inspire me to pursue my dreams. Loving thanks go to my dog, Digby, who sat beside me through hours of writing, editing, and proofing, and to the following people without whom this book could not be in your hands: my friends Laura Calloway for her invaluable advice and encouragement, Dave Bilinsky for his patience in reading my manuscript and for spotting errors concerning Canada's trust accounting rules, Tom Mighell and Allison Shields for their feedback and suggestions, and Jenni Claydon and Molly Montanaro of Lachina who competently and enthusiastically make good LP books happen. And last but not least, to ETHICSearch, the free legal ethics research service for members of the American Bar Association provided through the ABA Center for Professional Responsibility. Any errors in this book are mine alone.

INTRODUCTION

Getting Started

> *"If I were any good with numbers, I wouldn't have gone to law school."*
>
> *"If I don't have a client trust account, I won't get into trouble with the Bar."*

Sound familiar? Trust accounting may seem a daunting topic for a number of reasons. You may feel anxious about the idea of being solely responsible for safeguarding other people's money in your trust account. You may feel mathematically challenged when reviewing accounting reports or performing bookkeeping duties. You may even feel that the risk of doing something wrong and getting disbarred outweighs any benefit of getting money up front from clients.

All these feelings may become intensified during tough economic times, especially if you open your own law firm soon after becoming admitted to practice law. This was my experience in 2000, when I was admitted to the Oregon State Bar and the next day opened my law office and my IOLTA trust account. I haven't forgotten what those early days felt like. It doesn't matter how much experience you have practicing law or managing another type of business, opening a law practice, and becoming responsible for a trust account just seem fraught with peril.

This book is here to help this be less perilous for you. Since 2005 I have worked for the Oregon State Bar Professional Liability Fund as a practice management advisor, helping many lawyers understand how to fulfill their ethical duty to safeguard client and third-party property by properly setting up trust accounts and implementing best practices for managing them. By writing this book I hope to help you, too.

My goal is to explain this information simply and clearly so you will have less stress in setting up and managing your trust account and more enjoyment in running your own law firm. I hope you will mark up this book, so go ahead, gather your highlighters, pens, and Post-it flags, and let's begin.

Who Should Read This Book?

This book can serve as a quick overview and monthly go-to resource guide for lawyers and their staff who assist them in managing a trust account; for law professors and their students in a professional responsibility course during their discussions on handling a trust account; and for ethics counsel helping lawyers fulfill their ethical obligations to properly handle their trust account. To make this book relevant to the widest group of readers, we will look at both the American Bar Association Model Rules of Professional Conduct and the Federation Model Code of Professional Conduct from the Federation of Law Societies of Canada as general guidelines. Readers should treat the information in this book as a general overview and seek the relevant guidelines where they will practice.

In the field of law, trust accounting is an important topic, though the demands of mastering law as a profession and a business mean that there is limited time available for studying it. This book can become a valuable addition to your law library because it is one of the ABA Law Practice Division books in the One Hour for Lawyers series designed for today's busy law offices.

Understanding Your Ethical Obligations

To properly manage your trust account, you will need to be concerned with certain ethical obligations that are part of your jurisdiction's rules of professional conduct. We will focus on the American Bar Association Model Rules of Professional Conduct and the Federation Model Code of Professional Conduct from the Federation of Law Societies of Canada here, but you should consult the rules in your jurisdiction, as there may be additional or even different requirements that you must comply with.

Because fulfilling your ethical obligations is the foundation for properly managing your trust account, we will start with this topic in Lesson 1, on ethical obligations.

The prime ethical obligation is to properly safeguard the property belonging to your client or other third parties. In Lesson 2, we will look at safeguarding property.

Because this book's chief focus is trust accounting, in Lesson 3, we will review types of trust accounts, and in Lesson 4, we will look at the IOLTA program.

Day-to-Day Management of Your Trust Account

You do not need to understand any complicated accounting topics to properly manage your trust account or even to prepare accurate reports for your clients and other third parties.

You will be exposed to certain basis accounting concepts if you use an accounting program to handle your trust account. For example, you will want to know what a chart of accounts is and the difference between the accrual basis and cash basis of recordkeeping. In looking at available financial reports to generate, you will want to know about the income statement, balance sheet, and cash flow statement. In Lesson 5, we will cover accounting basics. For a more in-depth understanding of accounting, you will want to take a continuing legal education (CLE) class, read an accounting book, or consult an informative website such as accountingcoach.com.

Technology is very helpful with managing your trust account, and you will most likely buy software for this purpose. You will quickly see that the software can also track your general business account, so you will want to manage your law firm's business checking account with this same program. Before you know it, not only can you set up reports for tracking each subaccount for clients and third parties, but you can also generate helpful accounting reports that enable you to more effectively manage your law practice. Reports that would take hours for you to compile by hand are generated with a few clicks of the mouse and just as quickly printed on paper or as a PDF document and saved electronically in your report folders. In Lesson 6, we will cover technology for trust accounting.

To properly manage your trust account on a day-to-day basis, you will need to know how to open it and how to set up the subaccounts to track the funds that individual clients and others have entrusted to you. We will look at these topics in Lesson 7.

Proper management of your trust account will require you to know how to reconcile your trust account's monthly bank statement with your trust account checkbook register or journal of transactions and the individual transaction reports of each client subaccount on a consistent basis. These topics are discussed in Lesson 8.

You have an ethical obligation to report about funds you hold in your trust account. In Lesson 9, we will go over providing reports to clients and third parties.

Finally, you will need to know how to close your trust account when you no longer need to have one, whether this is because you are leaving the private practice of law or are joining an existing firm that has its own trust account. In Lesson 10, we will cover closing a trust account.

LESSON 1

Ethical Obligations

The ethical obligation to safeguard client and third-party property is explained in both the American Bar Association's (ABA's) Model Rules of Professional Conduct, Rule 1.15: Safekeeping Property; and the Federation of Law Societies of Canada's Federation Model Code of Professional Conduct, Code 3.5: Preservation of Clients' Property. This obligation is firmly rooted in fiduciary duty, the obligation to act in the best interest of another party, which has been the highest standard of care at equity or law since the time of the Court of Chancery in England (in a court of law, remedy to the prevailing party was that the losing party was compelled to pay fines and restitution, whereas in a court of equity, remedy to the prevailing party was that the losing party was compelled to take action or to cease action).

Today, the most recognized example of a fiduciary relationship is that between a lawyer and his or her clients, in which the lawyer owes fiduciary duties of loyalty and care to each client. The lawyer must exercise all the skill, care, and diligence of a professional fiduciary when acting on behalf of the client.

The No Commingling Rule

To prevent commingling of the lawyer's money with the money belonging to other people that is received during a representation, the lawyer must keep his or her own money in the law firm's operating or checking account and must keep all the money belonging to clients and third parties in a separate bank account, generally known as a trust account. Any money that the lawyer is holding for someone else belongs in a separate account from the lawyer's business and personal accounts. No exceptions are allowed. Throughout this book this account will be referred to as the trust account or client trust account.

Not every state and province follows the ABA's model rules on commingling funds. ABA Model Rule 1.15(b), which pertains to commingling, states that "a lawyer may deposit the lawyer's own funds in the trust account for the sole purpose of paying bank service charges on that account, but only in an amount necessary for that purpose." Oregon broadens this to allow the deposit of the lawyer's own funds into a trust account for paying bank service charges or meeting a minimum balance requirement, but only in amounts necessary for those purposes. In Canada, the Federation Model Code of Professional Conduct 3.5-4 states that "a lawyer must clearly label and identify clients' property and place it in safekeeping distinguishable from the lawyer's own property." In British Columbia, the Law Society permits a lawyer to hold up to $300 of the lawyer's own funds in the client trust account in order to have funds to offset the bank charges and small errors that occur from time to time and to prevent any negative balances. These examples show that it is wise to check with your particular jurisdiction before putting any of your own funds into your trust account.

Just as lawyers must not commingle their money with their client's money, they must not store client property intermixed with their own property. Thus, if important documents belonging to clients and third parties are being kept in a safe deposit box, this should be a separate safe deposit box from the safe deposit box where the law firm holds its own important papers.

Ethics Rules on the Duty to Keep Property Safely

Here are the rules issued on the topic of safeguarding property. Rules cited were current with the time of publication and are subject to change.

ABA Model Rule 1.15: Safekeeping Property (2016)

(a) A lawyer shall hold property of clients or third persons that is in a lawyer's possession in connection with a representation separate from the lawyer's own property. Funds shall be kept in a separate account maintained in the state where the lawyer's office is situated, or elsewhere with the consent of the client or third person.

(b) A lawyer may deposit the lawyer's own funds in a client trust account for the sole purpose of paying bank service charges on that account, but only in an amount necessary for that purpose.

(c) A lawyer shall deposit into a client trust account legal fees and expenses that have been paid in advance, to be withdrawn by the lawyer only as fees are earned or expenses incurred.

(d) Upon receiving funds or other property in which a client or third person has an interest, a lawyer shall promptly notify the client or third person. Except as stated in this rule or otherwise permitted by law or by agreement with the client, a lawyer shall promptly deliver to the client or third person any funds or other property that the client or third person is entitled to receive and, upon request by the client or third person, shall promptly render a full accounting regarding such property.

(e) When in the course of representation a lawyer is in possession of property in which two or more persons (one of whom may be the lawyer) claim interests, the property shall be kept separate by the lawyer until the dispute is resolved. The lawyer shall promptly distribute all portions of the property as to which the interests are not in dispute.

The comments that follow ABA Model Rule 1.15 are a reminder that lawyers should hold the property of others with the care of a professional fiduciary. A professional fiduciary who is holding money must keep accurate records of when funds were received on whose behalf and when paid on whose behalf, and this money should be held separately from the fiduciary's money.

Federation Model Code 3.5: Preservation of Clients' Property (2016)

Preservation of Clients' Property

3.5-1 In this rule, "property" includes a client's money, securities as defined in [provincial legislation], original documents such as wills, title deeds, minute books, licences, certificates and the like, and all other papers such as client's correspondence, files, reports, invoices and other such documents, as well as personal property including precious and semi-precious metals, jewellery and the like.

3.5-2 A lawyer must:

(a) care for a client's property as a careful and prudent owner would when dealing with like property; and
(b) observe all relevant rules and law about the preservation of a client's property entrusted to a lawyer.

Notification of Receipt of Property

3.5-3 A lawyer must promptly notify a client of the receipt of any money or other property of the client, unless satisfied that the client is aware that they have come into the lawyer's custody.

Identifying Clients' Property

3.5-4 A lawyer must clearly label and identify clients' property and place it in safekeeping distinguishable from the lawyer's own property.

3.5-5 A lawyer must maintain such records as necessary to identify clients' property that is in the lawyer's custody.

Accounting and Delivery

3.5-6 A lawyer must account promptly for clients' property that is in the lawyer's custody and deliver it to the order of the client on request or, if appropriate, at the conclusion of the retainer.

3.5-7 If a lawyer is unsure of the proper person to receive a client's property, the lawyer must apply to a tribunal of competent jurisdiction for direction.

The commentary to the Federation Model Code of Professional Conduct, Code 3.5, compares the duty of protecting client property to the duty of confidentiality in that the lawyer should take proper steps to ensure that the client property is protected from being viewed or accessed by people who do not have a right to view or access it. Thus, it would seem apparent that one should ensure that client property is protected from being wrongfully accessed.

Rules of Law Societies in Canada

The rules of the different law societies across Canada require that any trust funds be deposited as soon as possible. This makes good sense at any time because the safest place for money is in a bank.

> **Practice Tip:** *Promptly deposit whatever money you receive, especially cash, and secure other property upon receipt because you bear the burden of loss.*

Check your jurisdiction on whether this includes the duty to replace money and property wrongfully taken by hackers, embezzlers, and thieves. For example, see North Carolina's 2015 Formal Ethics Opinion 6, Lawyer's Professional Responsibility When Third Party Steals Funds from Trust Account: "Opinion rules that when funds are stolen from a lawyer's trust account by a third party who is not employed or supervised by the lawyer, and the lawyer was managing the trust account in compliance with the Rules of Professional Conduct, the lawyer is not professionally responsible for replacing the funds stolen from the account. NOTE: This opinion is limited to a lawyer's professional responsibilities and is not intended to opine on a lawyer's legal liability."

Ethical Handling of Disputes over Trust Account Disbursements

Because disputes happen, a lawyer needs to understand how to handle a dispute over a trust account disbursement. A dispute may arise if the client receives the monthly billing statement and questions part of the billed amount. If the lawyer has withdrawn funds from the client trust account under the fee agreement, upon learning that the client disputes a portion of the amount, the lawyer must put the amount that the client disputes back into the trust account.

If the funds have yet to be withdrawn from the trust account, the lawyer will need to withdraw only the amount that is not in dispute and leave the disputed amount in the client trust account.

As an example, Client A is charged for work by an associate on a project and also charged for the supervising partner's review of the associate's work; Client A then disputes being charged for the partner's time charges, believing these to be charges for training the associate, an administrative cost of the law firm. In this case, the law firm would put this disputed amount back into the client trust account until the dispute with Client A can be resolved.

Your bar association may have an alternative dispute resolution service that you may want to investigate and use, such as arbitration or mediation. If you use this service, include a provision about this dispute resolution process in your fee agreement so that by signing the fee agreement, the client agrees to the use of the alternate dispute resolution service in the event of a fee dispute.

Check with the rules of your jurisdiction. For example, the Rules of the Law Society of British Columbia provide a mechanism for a lawyer to follow when the client disputes the lawyer's right to claim funds in trust.

Practice Tip: ***Avoid many disputes with clients over fees and costs by clearly explaining all anticipated fees and costs up front.***

Other disputes may arise if a client does not understand his or her obligation to pay for certain costs, such as expert witness fees. Do not assume that your client will understand that this expert testimony is required to introduce evidence requiring scientific, technical, or specialized knowledge and that the expert witness will charge premium amounts for this testimony. The expert has specialized knowledge, skill, experience, training, or education that goes beyond that of the general population. It is important to explain that this expense of litigation is to be borne by the client. Ensuring that your client understands this prior to the commencement of the case will go a long way toward increasing your client's overall satisfaction with the outcome. If your client is using a lawyer for the first time, your client may have no frame of reference for determining what is a reasonable legal fee and legal cost. Be sure to discuss fees and costs up front before your client signs the engagement agreement allowing you to handle the legal matter.

Another source of dispute arises in a personal injury case if clients do not understand their insurance company's right to subrogation. *Subrogation* means that the insurance company has the right to pursue a third party that caused an insured loss to the insured as a means of recovering the amount the insurance company has paid to the insured for the loss. The insurance company expects to be reimbursed for paying the client's insured claims whenever a responsible third party is made to pay for damages. When medical damages are involved, the client's health insurance company will want to be reimbursed for the covered expenses paid.

Invariably, injured clients feel that they have diligently paid insurance premiums for years and should be entitled to having their expenses covered. When these injured clients find out at the time of settlement that their own medical insurance company is asking to be reimbursed for medical expenses paid on their behalf, they may feel this is unfair.

The same medical insurance company will not require reimbursement from another injured insured who had the same covered expenses but who did not win a personal injury settlement. By the time a personal injury case is settled, clients may be at the end of their rope and reluctant to endure anymore unpleasant surprises, like learning that a medical lien demanding repayment of coverage payments has been asserted against the settlement proceeds. Therefore, explain this subrogation obligation to your client before commencing litigation. Many lawyers can successfully negotiate a reduced amount to be repaid to the insurance company on behalf of their client. Although you cannot guarantee that you will be successful in doing this, your client will appreciate you for trying.

> **Practice Tip:** *Improve client communication by putting yourself in your client's shoes and addressing all issues that would seem confusing or unfair from a client's perspective. This requires you to think through a number of potential situations and then draft your fee agreement accordingly.*

Finally, do not become adversarial toward your client, or you will be in a self-conflict situation with that client in the event of a fee dispute or a bar complaint that you have charged or collected an unreasonable fee. Contact your bar's ethic counsel for advice, and you may need to suspend representing your client until the matter is resolved. Consider an evergreen fee agreement, which keeps money replenished in the trust account to ensure prompt payment of legal fees and costs. You want to avoid allowing money issues to become a source of aggravation to you or your client.

Should you wish to withdraw from representation based on nonpayment of funds into your trust account, you need to check the local rules that govern this procedure, whether you are in Canada or in the United States.

Ethics Rules on the Duty to Supervise Nonlawyers

Lawyers frequently have help in the day-to-day tasks of managing the trust account, such as preparing deposits to and withdrawals from the trust account, handling the bookkeeping responsibilities of recording all transactions, preparing statements to clients and third parties, and reconciling the trust account and client subaccounts to the monthly bank statement. You need to consult your jurisdiction's ethics rules to understand that you ultimately are responsible for any mistakes, ethical violations, or incidents of malfeasance of your employees or third-party services outside your firm. You must make reasonable effort to ensure that services are provided in a manner consistent with the lawyer's ethical obligations. Ultimate responsibility for the trust account cannot be delegated. The lawyer must maintain oversight. Model Rule 5.3 explains this responsibility to exercise care when delegating duties to support staff.

ABA Model Rule 5.3: Responsibilities Regarding Nonlawyer Assistance

With respect to a nonlawyer employed or retained by or associated with a lawyer:

(a) a partner, and a lawyer who individually or together with other lawyers possesses comparable managerial authority in a law firm shall make reasonable efforts to ensure that the firm has in effect measures giving reasonable assurance that the person's conduct is compatible with the professional obligations of the lawyer;

(b) a lawyer having direct supervisory authority over the nonlawyer shall make reasonable efforts to ensure that the person's conduct is compatible with the professional obligations of the lawyer; and

(c) a lawyer shall be responsible for conduct of such a person that would be a violation of the Rules of Professional Conduct if engaged in by a lawyer if:

  (1) the lawyer orders or, with the knowledge of the specific conduct, ratifies the conduct involved; or

  (2) the lawyer is a partner or has comparable managerial authority in the law firm in which the person is employed, or has direct supervisory authority over the person, and knows of the conduct at a time when its consequences can be avoided or mitigated but fails to take reasonable remedial action.

Comment

[1] Paragraph (a) requires lawyers with managerial authority within a law firm to make reasonable efforts to ensure that the firm has in effect measures giving reasonable assurance that nonlawyers in the firm and

nonlawyers outside the firm who work on firm matters act in a way compatible with the professional obligations of the lawyer. See Comment [6] to Rule 1.1 (retaining lawyers outside the firm) and Comment [1] to Rule 5.1 (responsibilities with respect to lawyers within a firm). Paragraph (b) applies to lawyers who have supervisory authority over such nonlawyers within or outside the firm. Paragraph (c) specifies the circumstances in which a lawyer is responsible for the conduct of such nonlawyers within or outside the firm that would be a violation of the Rules of Professional Conduct if engaged in by a lawyer.

NONLAWYERS WITHIN THE FIRM

[2] Lawyers generally employ assistants in their practice, including secretaries, investigators, law student interns, and paraprofessionals. Such assistants, whether employees or independent contractors, act for the lawyer in rendition of the lawyer's professional services. A lawyer must give such assistants appropriate instruction and supervision concerning the ethical aspects of their employment, particularly regarding the obligation not to disclose information relating to representation of the client, and should be responsible for their work product. The measures employed in supervising nonlawyers should take account of the fact that they do not have legal training and are not subject to professional discipline.

NONLAWYERS OUTSIDE THE FIRM

[3] A lawyer may use nonlawyers outside the firm to assist the lawyer in rendering legal services to the client. Examples include the retention of an investigative or paraprofessional service, hiring a document management company to create and maintain a database for complex litigation, sending client documents to a third party for printing or scanning, and using an Internet-based service to store client

information. When using such services outside the firm, a lawyer must make reasonable efforts to ensure that the services are provided in a manner that is compatible with the lawyer's professional obligations. The extent of this obligation will depend upon the circumstances, including the education, experience, and reputation of the nonlawyer; the nature of the services involved; the terms of any arrangements concerning the protection of client information; and the legal and ethical environments of the jurisdictions in which the services will be performed, particularly with regard to confidentiality. See also Rules 1.1 (competence), 1.2 (allocation of authority), 1.4 (communication with client), 1.6 (confidentiality), 5.4(a) (professional independence of the lawyer), and 5.5(a) (unauthorized practice of law). When retaining or directing a nonlawyer outside the firm, a lawyer should communicate directions appropriate under the circumstances to give reasonable assurance that the nonlawyer's conduct is compatible with the professional obligations of the lawyer.

[4] Where the client directs the selection of a particular nonlawyer service provider outside the firm, the lawyer ordinarily should agree with the client concerning the allocation of responsibility for monitoring as between the client and the lawyer. See Rule 1.2. When making such an allocation in a matter pending before a tribunal, lawyers and parties may have additional obligations that are a matter of law beyond the scope of these Rules.

In summary, a lawyer can use the services of nonlawyers inside and outside of the law firm so long as the lawyer ensures that the services are in keeping with the lawyer's professional obligations. To ensure this requires direct supervision or oversight. This requirement of direct supervision is addressed as well in the Federal Model Code governing Canadian lawyers, which follows.

Federation Model Code 6.1: Supervision

Direct Supervision Required

6.1-1 A lawyer has complete professional responsibility for all business entrusted to him or her and must directly supervise staff and assistants to whom the lawyer delegates particular tasks and functions.

Commentary

[1] A lawyer may permit a nonlawyer to act only under the supervision of a lawyer. The extent of supervision will depend on the type of legal matter, including the degree of standardization and repetitiveness of the matter, and the experience of the nonlawyer generally and with regard to the matter in question. The burden rests on the lawyer to educate a nonlawyer concerning the duties that the lawyer assigns to the nonlawyer and then to supervise the manner in which such duties are carried out. A lawyer should review the nonlawyer's work at sufficiently frequent intervals to enable the lawyer to ensure its proper and timely completion.

[2] A lawyer who practices alone or operates a branch or part-time office should ensure that

- *(a) all matters requiring a lawyer's professional skill and judgment are dealt with by a lawyer qualified to do the work; and*
- *(b) no unauthorized persons give legal advice, whether in the lawyer's name or otherwise.*

[3] If a nonlawyer has received specialized training or education and is competent to do independent work under the general supervision of a lawyer, a lawyer may delegate work to the nonlawyer.

[4] A lawyer in private practice may permit a nonlawyer to perform tasks delegated and supervised by a lawyer, so long as the lawyer maintains a direct relationship with the client. A lawyer in a community legal clinic funded by a provincial legal aid plan may do so, so long as the

lawyer maintains direct supervision of the client's case in accordance with the supervision requirements of the legal aid plan and assumes full professional responsibility for the work.

[5] Subject to the provisions of any statute, rule, or court practice in that regard, the question of what the lawyer may delegate to a nonlawyer generally turns on the distinction between any special knowledge of the nonlawyer and the professional and legal judgment of the lawyer, which, in the public interest, must be exercised by the lawyer whenever it is required.

The quote "trust, but verify," an old Russian proverb that President Ronald Reagan used during arms control, perfectly sums up lawyers' responsibility when delegating any duties concerning the management of their trust account.

LESSON 2

Safeguarding Property

Safeguarding Client Information

Trust accounting is only a small piece of safeguarding property. In the big picture, you hold much more than money belonging to your clients and third parties. Estate planning attorneys may hold original wills and trusts; real estate attorneys may hold original deeds and building permits; corporate attorneys may hold original stock certificates and corporate minute books; personal injury attorneys may hold photographs of injuries and the defective equipment that caused them, and the list goes on.

Personally Identifiable Information

No matter what your practice area, you hold client files containing personally identifiable information or sensitive personal information for each of your clients, such as name and address, date and place of birth, Social Security number (USA) or Social Insurance number (Canada), driver's license number, passport number, account numbers at financial institutions, and credit card numbers. Personally identifiable information is information that can be used on its own or with other information to identify, locate, or contact a person. Obviously, it must be safeguarded from falling into the wrong hands, meaning that we have a duty to protect our clients' most valuable possessions from becoming subject to identity theft.

Check with your jurisdiction regarding reporting requirements should there be a theft or unauthorized access of this protected information. For example, Rule 10-4 of the Rules of the Law Society of British Columbia has provisions on notifying the Society's executive director should you lose care and control of client documents.

You will want to check with your jurisdiction's bar regulatory agency as well as any statute or law that may require notification of a data breach affecting personal information. For example, Oregon's Data Breach Notification Law, which went into effect January 1, 2016, requires business and government agencies to notify the Oregon Attorney General's office when the personal data of at least 250 Oregonians have been compromised.

Other Information and Documents

What about other property? A fiduciary should protect property from being lost, damaged, or destroyed. Since lawyers frequently hold securities and other important documents, a professional fiduciary would keep these in a bank safety deposit box or some other proper receptacle, not in an unlocked, leaky shed behind rusting garden tools. Some have used such a shed and have been disciplined for their negligent handling of client property.

The important consideration is that the storage should be selected with care. Just putting original wills in manila folders in banker boxes in a storage room does not ensure that they will remain in pristine condition. If one lives in a wet climate, it becomes important that paper client files are stored in a humidity-controlled environment safe from mold and insects. Some law firms store original wills and other important documents in special fireproof safes instead of in a bank safe deposit box.

Be sure to keep an adequate and up-to-date inventory of all client property so that it can be located, identified, and returned. You are expected to keep such an inventory. Part of proper safeguarding is to create and maintain records of this property so that clients or third parties can be reunited with their property.

> **Practice Tip:** *Consider maintaining a scanned copy of all client documents that are in your care and store those data in a secure, off-site storage location, such as in a cloud backup, just in case a fire, flood, or natural or man-made disaster destroys the original documents.*

Safeguarding Money in a Trust Account

To properly safeguard money in your trust account, keep accurate records for each subaccount belonging to clients and third parties. Be careful, anytime you write a check from your trust account, to verify that the client has adequate funds to cover the check. Never just guess about your client's balance; verify it.

Ensuring the Money Is Actually in the Account

Be sure to wait until any funds deposited into the trust account are actually collected by your bank before making a disbursement. Otherwise you will be using money belonging to other clients. For example, if you deposit $10,000 from Mr. Jones into your trust account that held $50,000, you may think you have sufficient funds to immediately write a trust account check on behalf of Mr. Jones for $500. Your $500 check in reality is being withdrawn from the funds of your other clients because the funds from Mr. Jones have not yet been collected from his bank. This can happen when a lawyer confuses collected funds with available funds.

Whenever you make a deposit, your bank may indicate that a certain amount of money is available. It is. It was already in your trust account. "Funds are available" does not mean that your bank has received the funds from the issuing bank. The question to ask your bank is whether the funds have been collected from the issuing bank and deposited into your client trust account.

How long should you wait after depositing a check? Check with your state bar association's ethics counsel, with a practice management adviser for your bar or law society, or with your bank. Oregon recommends the 3-5-10 day rule. Allow three banking days for a check drawn on a local bank, five banking days for a check drawn on a bank in the same state, and ten banking days for a check drawn on a bank located out of state. A banking day is when a bank is open for conducting business, Monday through Friday except for any legal holidays. This protocol was worked out with the head of disciplinary services years ago, and local banks have not seen the need to change it. As long as you have and adhere to a policy of waiting a reasonable amount of time for various checks to be processed, you should be safe from inadvertent overdrafts caused by depositing a check that was not honored by the issuing bank.

Practice Tip: *Check with your local jurisdiction for best practice guidelines for developing your own protocol for when deposited funds can be used. Canadian practice advisers recommend calling your bank and following its directions with regard to how long to wait before a deposit has "cleared" the banking system to be reasonably certain that the funds are in your trust account.*

Protecting against Wrongful Access

Safeguarding the money in your trust account also includes protecting the means of accessing this account. Be sure to keep your supply of trust account checks and deposit slips in a locked drawer. They can be used to gain unauthorized access to the money you have been entrusted with. Because trust accounts usually hold a large amount of money, they are very attractive to thieves, fraudsters, and embezzlers. It is a bad idea, and may be forbidden in your jurisdiction to have an ATM account linked to your trust account.

In Canada, practice advisers recommend having your bank disable the ability to withdraw cash from your trust account via an ATM machine. Otherwise, it is too easy for funds to be wrongfully accessed.

Unfortunately, there have been instances of embezzlement of the trust account by a staff member who slips out to use the trust account ATM card to steal cash. Even if your bank imposes a limit on the cash amount available to be withdrawn via an ATM, you can get into serious trouble. If you don't monitor your trust account closely, you embolden the embezzler to repeat the act of embezzlement, so that it becomes a habit you won't discover until your trust account becomes overdrawn. The embezzler may be someone who comes into your office to help you with billing or may be someone who works for your bank and, from assisting you with your balance, has identified your trust account as not being closely monitored. Similarly, using signature stamps can facilitate embezzlement. It is dangerous to use a signature stamp, especially if it is not locked up and its use closely monitored. You can prove a forged signature but how could you prove wrongful use of a signature stamp? And if you engage in online banking for your trust account, be careful to have up-to-date anti-malware on your computer and use secure passwords lest a cybercriminal gain access to your trust account. We tend to worry about the security of the online banking site, when the real insecurity is in tracking malware on our computer.

Know of scams that involve your trust account. The use of counterfeit cashier checks is a popular way for fraudsters to steal trust account funds. Typically the counterfeit cashier check will be issued for a greater amount than necessary. The fraudster will demand an immediate refund of the funds paid in excess. By the time you discover that the cashier check is counterfeit, your fraudster is long gone with the money you refunded from the trust account. Always check with the issuing bank if there are any doubts or questions. Be on hyper alert for scams before a three-day bank holiday, which is a popular time to strike, and then avoid detection until after the banking holiday, by which time the fraudster is long gone.

Safeguarding Digital Property

Virtually every law firm uses a computer that holds digital property and from which it will send and receive e-mail and access the Internet. Most have a smartphone containing client e-mails and contact information. Many use cloud storage or cloud-based software on a subscription basis. Safeguarding this digital client property means understanding the proper measures to take to protect confidential client information from unauthorized access or attack. Cybersecurity is a critical topic as people scramble to address the increasing danger of being hacked; being infected by malware such as Trojans, worms, and key loggers; or becoming the latest victim of ransomware that holds digital data hostage until they pay the ransom for the decryption of locked data or the physical theft of a laptop, smartphone, or USB device.

If you elect to do online banking, it is important to consider that trust accounts frequently hold thousands of dollars and thus are highly attractive to cybercriminals. Ensure that you understand the dangers of accessing your trust account online, and take necessary safeguards to protect this account from unauthorized access. If your computer has become infiltrated by key logger malware, your password to access your trust account online could be captured by this spyware and used to steal money belonging to your clients and third parties. There has been at least one reported case of a law firm being targeted by a fraudster who was able to log into the firm's trust account.

Using Two-Factor Authorization

Whenever available, utilize two-factor authorization by combining something you have, such as a fingerprint, iris scan, or USB key, with something you know, such as a strong password or passphrase. You have been using two-factor authentication for years every time you have used an ATM machine: you must insert your physical ATM card and key in your PIN number before you can withdraw cash, make a deposit, or check your balance. You may also be using a two-step verification system such as Google Authenticator, which works with your Google Account and requires both a password and a code that the system sends to you as either a text message or an automated voice message. You may think this is equivalent to wearing a belt and suspenders; it's more equivalent to being tech savvy.

Staying Current with Technology

Technology is always changing, and it seems that every day we learn of another helpful new program or app that promises to save us time or improve our law practice. Some of these may not have all the kinks and flaws worked out before they are rushed to market. Others may appear innocuous but will install spyware into your computer. Take the time to research the company, read the terms of service and privacy policy, and evaluate whether there are specific vulnerabilities and risks that may arise before you press the download button. Understand specific ways to mitigate, if not eliminate, the risk of danger before you put your client's property in harm's way.

It is our ethical obligation to understand the technology that impacts our ability to provide competent legal services to our clients. Consider becoming actively involved with the ABA Law Practice Division to stay current on technology through informative articles, books, continuing legal education (CLE) classes, and the annual ABA TECHSHOW. Check the Resources section for further information.

Staying current with technology is important for attorneys in the United States and Canada. In the United States, Comment 8 of ABA Model Rule 1.1, Competence: Maintaining Competence, provides the following:

> [8] To maintain the requisite knowledge and skill, a lawyer should keep abreast of changes in the law and its practice, including the benefits and risks associated with relevant technology, engage in continuing study and education and comply with all continuing legal education requirements to which the lawyer is subject.

In Canada, the Model Code of Professional Conduct of the Federation of Law Societies of Canada states in its preface:

> The practice of law continues to evolve. Advances in technology, changes in the culture of those accessing legal services and the economics associated with practising law will continue to present challenges to lawyers. The ethical guidance provided to lawyers by their regulators should be responsive to this evolution. Rules of conduct should assist, not hinder, lawyers in providing legal services to the public in a way that ensures the public interest is protected.

Using Encryption

Safeguarding confidential client information means evaluating each situation to decide on the best practice under the circumstances. For example, you may use encryption programs such as PGP (Pretty Good Protection) or Symantec's Desktop Email Encryption when you are transmitting confidential information by e-mail, or VIIVO or Boxcryptor before storing client documents and files in cloud storage sites such as Google Drive, Dropbox, OneDrive, iCloud, and Box. Or maybe you want to turn on BitLocker, Microsoft's native file encryption program, which allows full disk encryption to protect your client data in case your Windows laptop gets lost while you are traveling, or turn on FileVault to encrypt the startup disk on your Mac. There are many products available in all categories of encryption programs. Look for current reviews before making up your mind about what available program is best for your needs, whether it is encryption for e-mail, full disk, or cloud storage. You have options.

Knowledge of encryption starts with understanding how it works. Encryption is the conversion of data into an unreadable format known as ciphertext that requires the use of a secret password or key that enables the ciphertext to be decoded or converted back into readable plain text. There are two categories of encryption: asymmetric and symmetric. In an asymmetric system, each party has a public key and each has a private key. The lawyer sends data encrypted with the recipient's public key. The recipient uses her private key to decrypt the message, and then uses the lawyer's public key to encrypt the reply so the lawyer can decrypt it with his private key. Conversely, the symmetric system utilizes just one key, a private key, for both encrypting and decrypting the message.

The first use of encryption has been attibuted to an Egyptian scribe who in the 1900s B.C.E. used nonstandard hieroglyphs in a secret inscription. It is still considered one of the most effective ways to ensure data security. But do more than secure data from unauthorized view or access; you have to secure it from complete destruction by having a secure current backup of your data.

If you use encryption, use it consistently. Dave Bilinsky, practice management adviser with the Law Society of British Columbia, once shared that a lawyer used to back up data on an encrypted portable hard drive. The lawyer forgot the hard drive one day and backed up the firm's data to an unencrypted flash drive, which was then lost. "A hard lesson to learn," said Dave, "and one that you don't wish to repeat. "

Trust but Verify

To safeguard digital property, you must be consistently diligent about securing it in all its forms. For example, smartphones are too often left unlocked so that they can be used quickly. And though many lawyers have backup systems in place for their computers, they trust instead of test. It is very important to conduct periodic test restores to check that your backup system is working.

Murphy's Law and the Blank Backup

Some law firms have found that there was a malfunction of the backup system when they needed to restore their data to the most recent backup. One firm discovered that the backup tapes locked in its vault had been blank for the past six months. No periodic test restores alerted them to this disaster. What can you afford to lose? You may want to back up daily and perform test restores weekly. One busy lawyer protested the cost and hassle of backing up her computer. She called me the next week and shared that her computer crashed but thanks to Carbonite, she was back up and running in fifteen minutes.

Have a policy that provides clear directions about handling all things digital. It should cover how to identify something suspicious and how to handle the malware that shows up in your inbox. You will find it extremely helpful to have protocols in place about dealing with unexpected attachments and hyperlinks in e-mails purporting to come from clients, colleagues, or companies, and train your staff to follow these protocols.

Using Strong Passwords to Protect Data

Another important way of safeguarding confidential information requires using strong passwords of 14 to 16 mixed-case letters, numerals, and symbols; changing them on a 30- or 60-day basis; and using a unique password for each required login. Too many people use the same passwords for multiple applications and do not change them frequently or at all. Using a passphrase may enable you to follow guidelines. For example, the phrase *My first car was a Mustard Yellow 1971 Volvo!* becomes the 15-digit passphrase *M1stcwaMY1971V!*

Securely Storing Passwords

There are always too many passwords to remember, and it is not safe to write them down and keep them next to your computer or on a Post-it note under your keyboard. It is helpful to use a secure password wallet or password manager, such as LastPass, KeePass, 1Password or RoboForm, or Keychain on a Mac, especially if it can generate sufficiently random passwords to use for websites. Writing passwords down in a notebook that you lock in a drawer or safe at night before going home is a dangerous practice because sooner or later the notebook will be lost or left out.

More about Cybersecurity

The days when we locked the outer door to our office and went home confident that client property was adequately protected are long gone. To learn more about cybersecurity, see the excellent resource *Locked Down: Practical Information Security for Lawyers*, Second Edition, by Sharon D. Nelson, David G. Reis, and John W. Simek (American Bar Association, 2016).

LESSON 3

Selecting Your Trust Account

In its most basic form, a trust account is an account in which you hold money belonging entirely or in part to clients or third parties for future use on their behalf. This may sound like you are like a bank and your clients and third parties are like depositors. However, in this situation, you control the money, not the depositors, and you need to send the depositors assurances that the money is safe.

Think for a minute how you would feel if you handed your money over to the bank and the bank exercised complete control of your money. It would make you nervous and you would want to receive timely statements showing all deposits into your account disclosing the date, source, amount, and purpose, as well as all withdrawals from your account disclosing the date, recipient, amount, and purpose. Depositors trust the bank to safeguard their money. You would expect the bank to keep accurate records of all the transactions and balances for each depositor and not get them all mixed up. When the bank reconciles the balances of all their depositor accounts, these individual accounts must equal the total money held on the books of the bank.

As a lawyer holding money belonging to your clients and third parties, you are indeed like a bank, and you have a duty to keep accurate records and to account or report to clients about their money, usually by issuing a statement monthly if there have been any transactions affecting their balance. As far as the bank is concerned, you have one trust account, but because you are holding money for more than one individual, you effectively have many trust accounts, tracked as one subaccount for each client and third party for whom you hold money.

Types of Accounts

There are various kinds of trust accounts. Check your jurisdiction for what type of trust account you must use for your clients. The most basic and oldest type is what is known as the pooled account. Prior to 1980, these pooled accounts were non-interest-bearing checking accounts. After federal banking laws in 1980 began to allow certain checking accounts to earn interest, if the amount held for the individual client was large enough or would be held long enough, the lawyer could put these funds into a separate interest-bearing account where the interest was paid to the client's benefit.

Because of administrative costs, however, it is impractical to open separate trust accounts that are for a small amount and held for a short time. Instead, the lawyer can use an interest-bearing pooled account for a group of clients if their deposits are sufficient in amount and duration to cover their allocated share of the cost for administering their funds, in which case the proportionate share of net interest is credited to the respective client or third party.

However, if a client has a large amount of money that would be held for a significant period of time, the lawyer can open an individual trust account on that client's behalf. It is important to note that a lawyer can never keep the interest earned on the trust account for the lawyer's personal benefit. It would be a violation of ethical and fiduciary duties to profit at the sake of your client.

The Pooled Interest-Bearing Trust Account

You might want to open a pooled interest-bearing trust account for several reasons. Maybe you have a group of clients who do not want to have their money generating interest that will be used to fund your state's Law Foundation or, in Canada, to fund the various Provincial Law Foundations. Or you may have a group of clients from a common group, such as members of an agricultural co-op or members of a homeowners' association. Or you may have identified a number of clients whose funds could earn sufficient interest to pay for the administrative costs of establishing and managing a pooled interest-bearing trust account for their benefit.

In this type of account, there are a number of clients with money pooled together, and each client's amount is tracked as a subaccount with the interest earned tracked and paid proportionally to each client, net of the prorated administrative costs, including bank service charges. You will need to report the interest earned by each client to the Internal Revenue Service at year end on a 1099-INT form. Check the requirements in your jurisdiction. In Canada, you would allocate the T5 Interest among the pooled account clients.

You will need to compute the interest earned by each client's trust fund and make payments to clients of their proportionate share of interest earned, net their proportionate share of bank charges. Interest earnings from a client trust account can never be used for the benefit of the law firm or lawyer personally.

This account should be set up under your federal Taxpayer Identification number: your Social Security (SS) number or Employer Identification number (EIN). Your role is as an interest nominee, earning interest that belongs to another. The financial institution reports the interest earned to the lawyer or law firm on the 1099-INT form, and the lawyer or law firm then reports the interest earned by each client on separate 1099-INT forms. The lawyer then sends these separate 1099-INT forms to each client and files a report to the IRS so that the IRS receives notice that the interest paid to the lawyer as an interest nominee has been paid properly to the clients.

You should title the name of the account XYZ Pooled Client Trust Account or something similar, subject to your jurisdiction's guidelines.

The IOLTA Account

What happens when the amount of client money is not large enough or held long enough to generate interest net any administrative costs? If a number of these small accounts of short duration are combined, together they can generate a net interest amount. Multiply this nominal interest by the number of local lawyer trust accounts holding small, short-term trust deposits, and the aggregated sum of all the net interest adds up to a sizable amount.

This money could be put to good use. In 1981, the Florida Bar Foundation established the first Interest on Lawyer Trust Accounts (IOLTA) program as a method of generating funds for charitable purposes, chiefly the funding of legal services to indigent persons with using interest earned on lawyer trust accounts identified as IOLTA accounts. It is a win-win situation because otherwise the potential interest is not available for anyone's benefit.

Client funds held in the client trust account in too small an amount and for too short a time to earn interest for the client, net administrative fees or bank charges, are placed together in an interest-bearing trust account in which the interest is transferred to the state's organization that runs the IOLTA program.

Today, IOLTA programs are operated by nonprofit law foundations in all U.S. states and in all Canadian provinces. These programs are an innovative means to increase access to justice for individuals living in poverty; they fund local nonprofit legal aid programs and support improvements to the justice system so that no one lacks access to our courts. Throughout the United States and Canada, most lawyers utilize the IOLTA trust account as their primary trust account. In some jurisdictions, participation in the IOLTA program is mandatory, and in others it is voluntary; check with your own jurisdiction.

For example, your jurisdiction may require that the lawyer open a separate interest-bearing trust account for any client whose funds are in a large enough amount and will be held for a long enough duration to earn enough interest to offset any account setup charges and costs of administering the account. Seek ethics advice to understand what your professional obligation will be in a situation where you have a client who can earn net interest but does not want to receive the interest. The language of the rule may state that the lawyer is obligated to open a separate interest-bearing trust account for this client. Note that if the jurisdiction requires the lawyer to open a separate interest-earning trust account for the client, then the lawyer must do so and cannot leave client funds in the IOLTA account that are expected to be of sufficient amount and duration to earn net interest. Check your jurisdiction because the phrase "a lawyer shall" means the lawyer is directed to do so.

You may think that the client could just waive the right to earning the net interest so that it goes to the IOLTA program. Unless a rule specifies that a client can waive a provision that a lawyer is directed to do, there can be no waiver. Oregon, which has a mandatory IOLTA program, states in the Oregon Rule of Professional Conduct 1.15-2:

> (b) All client funds shall be deposited in the lawyer's or law firm's IOLTA account unless a particular client's funds can earn net interest. All interest earned by funds held in the IOLTA account shall be paid to the Oregon Law Foundation as provided in this rule.
>
> (c) Client funds that can earn net interest shall be deposited in an interest bearing trust account for the client's benefit and the

net interest earned by funds in such an account shall be held in trust as property of the client in the same manner as is provided in paragraphs (a) through (d) of Rule 1.15-1 for the principal funds of the client. The interest bearing account shall be either:

(1) a separate account for each particular client or client matter; or

(2) a pooled lawyer trust account with subaccounting which will provide for computation of interest earned by each client's funds and the payment thereof, net of any bank service charges, to each client.

If you are not required to participate, should you bother to participate in your jurisdiction's IOLTA program and support access to justice? Should you say, "bah humbug" and just open a non-interest-bearing checking account to hold your trust account funds? Legal aid programs seek to serve the poor who otherwise would be denied their day in court because they cannot afford the cost of legal services. Do lawyers have a professional obligation to assist legal aid with adequate funding to carry out their mission? This is for you to decide, just as it is your decision whether to provide pro bono or reduced-rate legal services to those potential clients with limited or no resources. We will look at the IOLTA program in Lesson 4.

Check with your jurisdiction's IOLTA program to determine specific rules for opening an IOLTA. For example, lawyers in Canada must ensure that they send the letter of direction to their financial institution, directing it to forward all interest earned on the account to the respective law foundation in their province.

You will want to determine which financial institutions are authorized for opening IOLTA accounts. In Oregon, attorneys can only open IOLTA accounts with financial institutions that have contracted with the Oregon Law Foundation, outlining interest remittance and reporting requirements. In your jurisdiction, authorized financial institutions may include any that provide the level of depositor insurance, such as the

$250,000 per depositor from the Federal Deposit Insurance Corporation (FDIC) insurance in the United States; and that consents to transfer interest earned on the lawyer trust account to the jurisdiction's IOLTA program, as well as to get the lawyer's signed consent that the financial institution will promptly notify the jurisdiction's regulatory service if the lawyer trust account becomes overdrawn. Your jurisdiction may have specific requirements governing the proper way in which the IOLTA checking account should be titled, such as XYZ Client Trust Account, XYZ Lawyer Trust Account, or XYZ IOLTA Account.

The Taxpayer Identification number on this IOLTA account is the Taxpayer Identification number associated with your state's IOLTA program because that is the recipient of the interest income to be earned.

> **Practice Tip:** *To ensure that your law firm IOLTA account can always be accessed in the event of your disability or death, you will want to have a second authorized signer on the IOLTA account. Check your jurisdiction for regulations regarding authorized signatories on an IOLTA account. For example, in Washington, only a lawyer can be an authorized signatory on an IOLTA account, while Oregon does not have this requirement.*

The Separate Interest-Bearing Trust Account

You may need to open a separate interest-bearing client trust account for a particular client or client matter when the client could earn net interest. Typically, you will open one of these accounts when your jurisdiction requires that if a client could earn net interest, that client should have a separate trust account where interest earned belongs to that client.

Accordingly, name this account Client Trust Account for Client XYZ. Some jurisdictions will require you to use your federal Taxpayer Identification number (SS number or EIN) and, as with the pooled account where you serve as an interest nominee, you will issue the client a 1099-INT form. Other jurisdictions will insist that you use the client's SS number on this account so that interest is reportable to the client. Check with your jurisdiction for the proper procedure.

> **Practice Tip:** *Check your jurisdiction's requirement regarding which Taxpayer Identification number should be used on the individual interest-bearing trust account. For example, in Washington, the account is set up using the client's Taxpayer Identification number but the attorney is the signer on the account, while in Oregon the Taxpayer Identification number should be the law firm's Taxpayer Identification number.*

When Can a Client Earn Net Interest?

To determine whether your client could earn net interest, consider the following factors:

1) The amount of the funds to be deposited
2) The expected duration of the deposits
3) The rate of interest at financial institutions where the funds are to be deposited
4) The cost of establishing and administering a separate interest-bearing client trust account for the client's benefit, including the bank's service charges and the administrative costs for the law firm to handle this account, including the cost of preparing the tax-related documents (1099s) to report to the IRS and account to the client for income accruing to the client's benefit
5) The capability of the financial institution and the lawyer or law firm to calculate and pay income to individual clients
6) The likelihood of any other circumstances that affect the ability of the client's funds to earn a net return of interest for the client

If you are required to monitor your client trust account to determine whether any client could earn net interest and therefore needs a separate interest-bearing client trust account, you may encounter a situation where you discover that a client is entitled to a separate trust account because of earning net interest. You would then request a refund of interest for this client from your state's IOLTA program, if your state's IOLTA program allows for this. This likely is not allowed in Canada. My colleague Dave Bilinsky from the Law Society of British Columbia has not heard of requesting a refund of interest once paid over to the Law Foundation. Check before attempting to request a refund of interest that should have accrued to a particular client.

> **Practice Tip:** *Calculate whether your client's funds would produce a positive net return of interest: interest = principal × interest rate/12 × number of months. For example, $10,000 deposit at 5 percent interest for one month would earn $41.67 ($10,000 × .05/12 × 1 = $41.67). Compare this amount to the cost of the law firm's time to open the account, for example, $25 plus the bank's monthly maintenance fee of $7.50. The client would earn a positive net return of $9.17 ($41.67 – $25 – $7.50 = $9.17).*

Can your client waive the interest? Maybe. Check with your jurisdiction. Your client may be allowed to waive the right to interest earned on funds held in the IOLTA on the client's behalf. If allowed, this is essentially a charitable contribution, and the client should be so informed by the lawyer and encouraged to seek independent tax advice before deciding how to proceed.

Be careful if you choose to advise your client on this point, as you may have a self-interest conflict under Rule 1.7(a)(2) for giving this advice, and then must obtain the client's informed consent in accord with Rule 1.7(b). The self-interest conflict arises because if the client follows your advice, you will be saved expending the time and effort of setting up a separate trust account so that the client is paid the net interest earned. With these steps followed, the lawyer may, with the client's agreement, deposit the client's funds into the IOLTA account.

Other Accounts for Safeguarding Clients' Money

There are a few other instances when you might hold money belonging to someone else. You may be acting in dual roles, as the lawyer and as the executor or administrator of an estate, or as the lawyer and as the conservator of a legally protected person, someone who is deemed by the court as being unable to protect his or her property, such as a child or sufficiently disabled adult. If this situation arose out of an attorney-client or solicitor-client relationship, some jurisdictions would consider them to be trust accounts, while others might classify them as probate accounts and conservatorship accounts, no different from the probate accounts being handled by a different executor/administrator for whom you are the representing attorney or conservatorship accounts being handled by a different conservator for whom you are the representing attorney.

Both of these accounts would be considered trust accounts in Canada and would be dealt with in the same manner if they arose out of a solicitor-client relationship. They may or may not be interest-bearing, depending on specific factors. Additionally, lawyers in Canada may also operate a separate trust account for the purposes of remitting fees and taxes for electronic registration of documents in various registries in each province.

Practice Tip: *If you have money belonging to a client or third party that arises out of the attorney-client or solicitor-client relationship, check with your jurisdiction if there is any question on whether it belongs in a trust account.*

LESSON 4

Understanding the IOLTA Program

The IOLTA is for holding client money that is in too small an amount for too short a time to be able to earn interest net any administrative costs of having a separate trust account for each client. The lawyer cannot keep the interest accruing to the collective clients' funds. Rather than having a non-interest-bearing account, lawyers can set up IOLTA accounts where the interest accruing to the collective client funds is transferred to the nonprofit law foundation for administering the state or providence's IOLTA program. Depending on your jurisdiction, you may be required to participate, may elect to participate, or may elect to opt out of participation. It is not possible to opt out in Canada.

Benefits of the Program

The IOLTA program has been adopted by every jurisdiction and is a wonderful way to support access to justice. The collected interest accumulated in all of the participating IOLTA accounts provides legal services to persons of lesser means and funds for educating the public about the law.

Educating the public about the law in your jurisdiction may include supporting education programs such as Law Day in the United States, for celebrating the rule of law and its contribution to the freedoms enjoyed by Americans, and the Classroom Law Project, for teaching kindergarten through grade 12 students how to become active citizens.

Providing legal services to persons of lesser means in your jurisdiction will likely involve a nonprofit organization known as legal aid that provides free legal services in various categories, such as debtor relief; domestic relations including divorce, modification of support, antistalking orders, consumer rights, appeals of administrative rulings and denial of benefits; and assistance with landlord tenant law. It is important to realize that even though your jurisdiction has financial need thresholds for determining who can access the legal aid services, it probably has far more people who qualify for legal aid services than the legal aid offices can provide.

> **Practice Tip:** *If the thought that there is greater need of legal services to the poor and disadvantaged concerns you, contact your local bar association to find out how you can help by providing pro bono services.*

History of the Program

The first IOLTA program was in Florida in 1981, and now all 50 states, plus the District of Columbia and the Virgin Islands, operate IOLTA programs. A number of Canadian jurisdictions, including Alberta, British Columbia, Manitoba, New Brunswick, Newfoundland and Labrador, Northwest Territories, Nova Scotia, Nunavut, Ontario, Prince Edward Island, Quebec, Saskatchewan, and Yukon, also operate their own successful programs. How successful are they? Since the IOLTA program became mandatory in 1989, the Oregon Law Foundation has awarded over $29,000,000 for charitable, law-related purposes. The existence of IOLTA has allowed the Oregon Law Foundation to fund programs that provide civil legal services to people of lesser means, helping to create greater access to justice in Oregon. See http://www.oregonlawfoundation.org/history.html. Each state and province can likely boast similar success stories. To find a listing of all these programs with their contact information, see the American Bar Association's Directory of IOLTA Programs at http://www.americanbar.org/groups/interest_lawyers_trust_accounts/resources/directory_of_iolta_programs.html#CN.

The ABA Commission on Interest on Lawyers' Trust Accounts and the National Association of IOLTA Programs report on the Commission's webpage that in 2008 IOLTA grants totaled $263.4 million nationwide (http://www.americanbar.org/groups/interest_lawyers_trust_accounts/overview.html). Close to 90 percent of IOLTA grants go to provide a significant source of funding for legal aid offices and various pro bono programs. Your state IOLTA program can provide you with information about how these funds are benefiting the public in your state.

IOLTA programs vary. Currently in South Dakota and the Virgin Islands, they are voluntary and lawyers must affirmatively choose to participate. In Alaska, Kansas, Nebraska, and Virginia, they are opt-out programs in which all lawyers participate unless they affirmatively choose not to. In the remaining states, the District of Columbia, and Puerto Rico, they are mandatory, and all lawyers in the jurisdiction who maintain client trust accounts must participate.

Litigation Regarding IOLTA Programs

There has been litigation challenging the constitutionality of the IOLTA programs in Texas and Washington, but both cases were heard in the U.S. Supreme Court in *Phillips, et al. v. Washington Legal Foundation, et al.*, 524 U.S. 156, 118 S Ct 1925 (1998), and *Brown v. Legal*

Foundation of Washington, 538 U.S. 216 (2003). The Supreme Court upheld the constitutionality of the IOLTA program under the Just Compensation Clause of the Fifth Amendment.

Deposit Insurance on IOLTA Accounts

Historically, credit unions could not offer IOLTA accounts because of the way in which deposits in credit unions were insured by the federal government. Only bank accounts covered by the Federal Deposit Insurance Corporation (FDIC) would qualify. Toward the end of 2014, the U.S. Senate passed the Credit Union Share Insurance Fund Parity Act, which provides the same level of insurance coverage as for IOLTA accounts held at banks. President Obama signed the Credit Union Share Insurance Fund Parity Act into law on December 18, 2014, and now credit unions may offer IOLTA accounts to lawyers.

In the United States, all IOLTA accounts now have $250,000 of protection per person per institution, assuming the account is properly designated as a trust account at the financial institution and the law firm maintains a proper accounting of each client and third party's funds held within the account.

In Canada, the Canadian Deposit Insurance Corporation (CDIC) covers accounts with national banks. Trust accounts with credit unions are covered by the respective province's legislation established for the insurance of accounts. Lawyers must ensure that they comply with any annual notice provisions to their financial institution if they want each client's deposit in a pooled trust account to be covered for the maximum insurance coverage that is offered, rather than having one limit shared among all clients.

Lawyers should let their clients know in which financial institution their trust account is established. This may be an issue for clients with significant balances in the same financial institution because funds held in excess of the maximum $250,000 deposit insurance limit per account ownership will not have FDIC or National Credit Union Administration (NCUA) insurance coverage.

Clients Who Can Earn Net Interest

As covered in Lesson 3, if you are holding a sufficient amount of money for a sufficient length of time that a client can earn net interest on the amount deposited after the bank's and law firm's administrative fees are deducted, you may be required to deposit the funds in an interest-bearing client trust account for the client's benefit.

Lawyers have an affirmative duty to monitor the IOLTA account at regular intervals. If you determine that a particular client's funds have been significant enough to earn net interest, you should check with your state's IOLTA program about whether your client should have a separate interest-earning trust account or whether you should get signed client consent for donating the client's interest earned to your state's IOLTA program.

Consult your state rules of professional conduct or contact your state's ethics counsel for guidance about the client who could earn net interest. The IOLTA program anticipates that client funds held in a trust account will be such a small amount or held for such a short duration that any interest earned will be negligible.

If your jurisdiction requires that clients who can earn net interest be given their net interest and the client's funds have been held in your IOLTA account, you will need to check with your jurisdiction before proceeding. In Oregon, you are required to request a refund from the Oregon Law Foundation for any interest earned by the client's funds that was transferred to the IOLTA program.

Providing Notice to Your Client

Be sure to notify your clients that interest earned on the sums in your client trust account is transferred to your state's IOLTA program. Display a sign in your office, provide brochures, or include a statement on your fee agreement or monthly billing statement. Most clients are proud that this innovative program allows the legal profession to help those who otherwise cannot afford access to justice. The interest on all these IOLTA accounts becomes a significant way of funding charitable, law-related programs that provide civil legal services to people of limited means, such as legal aid programs and law-related educational programs for the general public.

LESSON 5

Accounting Basics

If you have decided to use software to help you manage your trust account, you have already been exposed to certain accounting principles, concepts, and reports. Many lawyers running their own law firms find themselves pushed into an understanding of accounting principles early on by their accountants or colleagues who have already established their own law office. They are usually encouraged to keep proper track of their client trust account with an accounting software program such as QuickBooks, and if they are going to go through the exercise of setting up their trust account information using QuickBooks, they may as well use it to manage their law firm's general account to track income and expenses and track profitability.

The first employee the busy new practice hopes to hire is a bookkeeper. But however smart your bookkeeper and accountant are, you must remain mindful of your ethical obligation to provide adequate supervision of staff and others, to oversee that trust accounting is being done properly and that all property entrusted to you is being safeguarded. This is actually not too difficult.

Practice Tip: *Though Excel and other spreadsheet programs are helpful in the law office, they are not acceptable accounting systems because they lack many important features of a proper accounting system, such as trust audit trails and proper double-entry accounting.*

Basic Accounting Terminology

First, let's get some of the accounting terminology out of the way. Accounting is concerned with three things: assets, liabilities, and owner's equity.

Assets and Liabilities

Assets are what you own. Examples include current assets that will be used up or turned into cash within a year, such as cash, accounts receivable, and prepaid costs that are still of value, such as prepaid advertising, prepaid insurance, and prepaid rent. They also include long-term assets such as investments, land, buildings, improvements, equipment, and furniture and intangible assets such as goodwill, trade names, and trademarks.

Liabilities are what you owe. Examples include notes or loans payable, accounts payable, salaries and wages payable, interest payable, and the trust account, which represents money you are holding for others and will have to pay at some future time. Liabilities are categorized as current liabilities if the obligation is due right now.

The money in your client trust account represents an obligation; it must be returned to the rightful owners, your clients, and other third parties for whom you hold money. Should they ask for the return of their money, if it is not already earned by you, that money is due now. Thus, your client trust account is tracked both as *Bank Account (CASH)—CLIENT TRUST ACCOUNT* and as *Other Current Liability—CLIENT TRUST ACCOUNT*, where you will track subaccounts, one for each client trust account. The first account equals the second; the second is the sum of all subaccounts.

How This Accounting Works

The following should help show how this works in practice:

> At Local Bank, you open a *Law Firm General Operating Account*, a business checking account for managing the money

belonging to your law firm from which you pay all business expenses and to which you deposit all business income. You also open a *Client Trust Account* for managing the money belonging to your clients separately, from which you pay legal fees and costs as incurred by your client and to which you deposit any money received on behalf of your client, such as settlement proceeds.

In your law firm accounting software program, you would set up two bank accounts for managing your new accounts: a *Law Firm General Operating Account*, which is a Bank Account (CASH), and a *Client Trust Account*, which is also a Bank Account (CASH).

Three new clients pay you advanced legal fees and costs totaling $10,000: Client A $3,000, Client B $4,000, and Client C $3,000. You deposit this $10,000 into your *Client Trust Account* held at Local Bank.

1. In your law firm accounting software program, you set up three subaccounts under *Other Current Liability—CLIENT TRUST ACCOUNT*: Subaccount Client A; Subaccount Client B; and Subaccount Client C.
2. You enter the $10,000 deposit in the *Bank Account (CASH)—CLIENT TRUST ACCOUNT.*
3. You allocate $3,000 to *Other Current Liability—CLIENT TRUST ACCOUNT*, Subaccount Client A; $4,000 to Subaccount Client B; and $3,000 to Subaccount Client C.
4. You have done this correctly if the *Bank Account (CASH)—CLIENT TRUST ACCOUNT* has a balance of $10,000 and the *Other Current Liability—CLIENT TRUST ACCOUNT* has a balance of $10,000 with subaccounts showing balances of Client A with $3,000, Client B with $4,000, and Client C with $3,000.

Client B decides not to pursue the legal matter so fires you before any work has been done. You write a check from the Local Bank *Client Trust Account* for $4,000 payable to Client B to refund all the money paid but unearned.

1. In your law firm accounting software program, you log this transaction as a $4,000 withdrawal from the *Bank Account (CASH)—CLIENT TRUST ACCOUNT.*
2. You allocate this $4,000 to the *Other Current Liability—CLIENT TRUST ACCOUNT*, Subaccount Client B.
3. You have done this correctly if the *Bank Account (CASH)—CLIENT TRUST ACCOUNT* has a balance of $6,000 and the total of *Other Current Liability—CLIENT TRUST ACCOUNT* has a balance of $6,000 with subaccounts Client A $3,000, Client B $0, and Client C $3,000.

Owner's Equity

Owner's equity is the difference between assets and liabilities. Here is the accounting equation that expresses this relationship:

Assets = Liabilities + Owner's Equity or Shareholder's Equity

This equation will always be in balance if you keep accurate records. The collection of all the company's financial records is maintained in the general ledger that includes accounts for assets, liabilities, owners' equity, revenues, and expenses. The accounting equation's left side should always equal the right side. Balance is maintained because every business transaction affects at least two of your law firm's accounts.

Thankfully, software to handle accounting is readily available and incredibly affordable as well as extremely important. Because you are safeguarding money that belongs to clients and other third parties, you need to keep track. The burden of doing this with pencil and ledger paper decides of using accounting software a no-brainer.

Your law firm will need to keep track of all its transactions by recording them in the correct account in its general ledger. These accounts are identified in the chart of accounts.

The Chart of Accounts

The names of the accounts used for reporting financial transactions are found in the chart of accounts, which provides the category names for your firm's expenses, revenues, assets, and liabilities. If using accounting software, you will be provided with a sample chart of accounts for a service business or law firm. Because these are samples, you will want to make adjustments to the chart of accounts so that the names of these accounts are most suitable for your specific law firm practice. Your accountant can help you with this.

Again, the cost of accounting software is so reasonable that no law firm keeps track of transactions manually. In these software applications, entry making is so easy that most programs automatically debit or credit the cash account when a check or deposit is recorded. Dual-entry bookkeeping is not a problem because the concept is built into your program and you just need to ensure that all transactions are recorded promptly and adequate reports to track the funds for each client subaccount are set up.

Summary So Far

To summarize, when you first set up your accounting program, you will set up a *Bank Account (CASH)—GENERAL OPERATING ACCOUNT* and a *Bank Account (CASH)—CLIENT TRUST ACCOUNT* for managing your law firm's Business Checking Account and your law firm's Client Trust Account. The money in the Client Trust Account belongs to your clients and any third parties, because you will need to repay that money at any time your client asks for it; it is tracked as *Other Current Liability—CLIENT TRUST ACCOUNT*, with each client set up as a separate subaccount. The balance of the overall *CLIENT TRUST ACCOUNT* will always equal the sum of all the individual Client Subaccounts. You need these subaccounts for monitoring money being held for each client and other third party.

Don't forget that if your jurisdiction allows or requires you to keep a nominal amount of your law firm's money in your client trust account for paying bank service charges as they are automatically deducted from the account, you will need to set up a subaccount for your law firm to keep track of these funds: *Other Current Liability—CLIENT TRUST ACCOUNT: Subaccount—Law Firm Bank Charges*. Otherwise, your *Other Current Liability—CLIENT TRUST ACCOUNT* will not balance the *Bank Account (CASH)—CLIENT TRUST ACCOUNT.*

The important thing to remember is that the client trust account is money in the bank, but it is not your money, and though it is a Bank Account (CASH), it not your asset. It is money that belongs to others and would be currently owing to them; thus it needs to be categorized as an "Other Current Liability."

To help you set up your law office accounting system, please see Appendix D for a sample chart of accounts for a law firm.

Introduction to Basic Accounting

The three most important financial statements are the *income statement*, the *balance sheet*, and the *statement of cash flows*. These reports will help you run a profitable law practice, and if you plan to get a business loan, you will need to provide current reports to your business loan officer. Luckily, if you have an accounting software program, you will be able to generate these reports easily because the program will help you correctly record your financial transactions.

Financial Statement: The Income Statement

The income statement is important because it shows how profitable your law firm has been during the time period shown in the statement's heading, typically for the month, the quarter, or the year. Select the starting and ending dates for whatever time period you choose to review. You will be able to see your financial trends by reviewing your income statement on a quarterly basis and comparing these quarterly income statement reports to each other.

You'd think, since it is called an income statement, that this first report would record cash coming into your law firm. Welcome to the world of accounting. In reality, the income statement's purpose is to report the profitability of your law firm (by reporting the revenues *earned* by your law firm's efforts during the reported time period) and to report the expenses *incurred* by the law firm during that same time period. The difference between income and expenses is stated as net income or net loss and is commonly referred to as the "bottom line."

When first setting up your accounting program, you will be asked how you keep your business books, on a cash basis or accrual basis. Most law firms in the United States elect cash basis, but you should understand what these two options are so that you make the choice that makes sense to you. All law firms in Canada operate under the accrual basis. Accordingly, Canadian law firms must ensure that they are using an accounting system written for Canada, as otherwise they could find themselves with financial books and records that are not being kept in accordance with Canadian tax and accounting requirements.

Accrual Basis of Accounting

Under the *accrual basis* of accounting, revenues are recorded when they are earned (i.e., when the work is completed and the bill is sent), not when the law firm receives the money. Essentially, you have accrued the right to income. A business using the accrual basis of accounting recognizes income when the right to that income occurs, when it is earned.

It is important to realize the tax ramifications of being on the accrual basis. Because you have recognized the income when you accrued the right to receive that income, you are taxed as if you had already received the income. Certainly you will later make an adjustment for the bad debt if the client does not pay. The point here is that your liability for tax is when the income is recognized, which is when the right to it accrues, even if you do not yet have the money in hand.

Under the accrual basis, an expense is recognized when the obligation to pay that expense is incurred. Because of the matching principle, the expense is recorded with the matching revenue. Most manufacturing businesses use the accrual method of accounting because it better illustrates profitability by matching expenses with the income those expenses helped to generate.

Cash Basis of Accounting

In the *cash basis* of accounting, income is recognized when the income is actually received, and expense is recognized when the expense is actually paid. Under the cash basis of accounting, revenues are recorded when they are received, not when they are earned by the law firm. A business using the cash basis of accounting recognizes income only when payment is received.

It is important to realize the tax ramifications of being on the cash basis. Because you only recognize the income as you receive the money, you are only liable for income tax if you have received the income. Thus your liability for tax is when the income is actually received. The downside of the cash method is that profitability on a particular matter is harder to determine because it may take place months, or even years, before income from that matter is received.

Many lawyers setting up their accounting software elect to set up their books on the cash basis because that is what is most familiar. We run our personal finances on a cash basis and prepare our personal income tax returns based on how much we were paid and how much we paid in deductible expenses. Income is when we receive our paycheck. Expense is when we pay our mortgage.

The Choice of Accrual or Cash Basis

Currently, the law allows all U.S.-based law firms to use the cash method of accounting for tax purposes. There is a push in Congress to have all law firms with annual gross receipts over $10 million to use the accrual method of accounting rather than the traditional cash receipts and disbursement method. As the ABA points out in its ABA Fact Sheet, updated in April 2016,

> Section 3301 of H.R. 1, introduced during the 113th Congress, and Section 51 of a similar draft bill prepared by the Senate Finance Committee staff would require all such businesses with annual gross receipts over $10 million to use the accrual method of accounting rather than the traditional cash receipts and disbursements method.

See more about this in the post "Mandatory Accrual Accounting for Law Firms": http://www.americanbar.org/content/dam/aba/uncategorized/GAO/accrualaccountingfactsheet.authcheckdam.pdf. The ABA and many state and local bars have voiced objections to the legislation. Mandating reporting on an accrual basis will force firms to pay taxes on income when earned instead of when paid, if paid; hence the outcry of paying taxes on "phantom income."

Most businesses in Canada are required to use the accrual basis for preparing accounting records; however, under S. 34 of the Income Tax Act, professional businesses (accountants, dentists, lawyers, medical doctors, veterinarians, and chiropractors) may use a modified accrual basis, where work in progress is not included in revenue. In Canada, revenue is recognized at the time lawyers render an invoice, not when they accrue work in progress (WIP).

Is one method better than the other? The benefit of the accrual basis is that it is a precise reflection of how a business operates. Looking at your firm's finances on an accrual basis of reporting gives a clear picture of what it takes to generate each revenue because expenses are matched to their associated revenues. The benefit of the cash basis is that it is a simple system that is already familiar because we tend to run our personal finances on a cash basis of actual receipt of income and payment of expenses.

Financial Statement: The Balance Sheet

The balance sheet is important because it provides a snapshot of your law firm's financial position at a given point in time, typically at the end of the month, the end of the quarter, or the end of the year. It can be whatever point in time you need a snapshot. You will see more of your financial trends by reviewing them on a quarterly basis.

The balance sheet will only show where things stand on a specific date. It reports the law firm's assets, liabilities, and the owner's equity or stockholders' equity at a specific point in time as opposed to over time.

If you are looking at your law firm's balance sheet dated December 31, then the amounts shown are the balances in the accounts after all transactions pertaining to December 31 have been recorded.

Financial Statement: The Statement of Cash Flows

The statement of cash flows is important because it shows how your law firm's cash amount has changed during the time interval in the statement's heading.

For planning purposes, it is helpful to be able to see the cash generated and used by the law firm's operating activities, any investing activities, and any financing activities.

Like the income statement, the statement of cash flows is concerned with a time interval rather than a point in time, typically for the month, the quarter, or the year. Select the starting and ending dates for whatever time period you review. You will see more of your financial trends by reviewing them on a quarterly basis. If you operate your firm on the cash basis, your statement of cash flows and your income statement will be essentially the same. If you operate on an accrual basis, the statement of income and expenses provides a clearer picture of actual cash flows.

Your biggest role will likely be monitoring the monthly reports of your law firm's income and expenses and monitoring the monthly reports for each client or third party's subaccount in your trust account. You must be able to properly monitor the accuracy of any reports pertaining to your trust account even if they are prepared by a trained bookkeeper because you cannot delegate the full responsibility for the trust account. You remain ultimately responsible for your client trust account.

LESSON 6

Technology for Trust Accounting

In the old days, scribes wrote books out by hand. We had very few books and they were expensive because they were so labor-intensive to produce. Technology has changed that. Book printing has evolved. Likewise, we wouldn't dream of writing a client letter or court pleading using a typewriter, manual or electric. Trust accounting in the old days required laborious work of keeping a ledger for the overall account and then transferring each entry to an individual ledger card for each client or third party on which to write down all deposits to and withdrawals from the trust account on behalf of that individual.

Technology has changed this process of trust accounting, making it faster to maintain and making it more accurate. You make the entry once, indicating the appropriate client matter, and the software automatically makes the additional entries needed on the appropriate individual client ledger. Software that can handle trust accounting is not that expensive. You will recoup the cost of purchasing this software quickly because you will not be spending as much time doing it by hand.

Deciding on Software and Services

Basically, any accounting software program can be used for managing your trust accounting. There is one major caution about using

QuickBooks for trust accounting: you can change a transaction in these programs without leaving a trace. This means someone could alter a transaction without being detected. A full-featured accounting program that would be used in a financial institution would generate a paper trail of all changes to transactions, and there would be checks and balances in place. Obviously this level of security is critical in an environment where there are a number of people who have access to the program. If you are a solo, this will be less of a concern because you are likely the only person entering transactions.

Many software programs are specifically designed for law firms. These programs will already have the typically legal costs included. The chart of accounts sets forth the various categories of income and expenses. If this is a legal-specific program, you will see the familiar law firm–related accounts listed, such as legal services, advanced costs, court-filing fees, expert witness fees, court reporting fees, deposition service, and process service.

Some case management programs are all-in-one programs to cover both the front and back office, such as calendaring, docketing, time-keeping, billing, and trust accounting. Other programs offer individual components to be purchased, such as payroll.

The ABA Legal Technology Resource Center provides a Practice/Case Management Software Comparison Chart for Solos/Small Firms and a Time and Billing Software Comparison Chart for Solos/Small Firms that include those programs that provide trust accounting features. The biggest decision to make is whether you want software that resides on your computer or whether you want to use a cloud-based program. Many programs of both varieties also include a mobile app for tracking time and costs on the fly. Be sure to take advantage of 30-day trial periods, and set aside time to put the program to use;

otherwise you might end up with an expensive program you will not use.

Canadian lawyers should ensure that their choice of program either keeps accounting records in accordance with Canadian accounting and tax requirements or works with an accounting system that does so.

Some Programs to Review

Most programs are Web- or cloud-based, offered on a subscription basis. If cloud-based, be sure to review the terms of service and privacy agreement and security features, including backup of your data. You should be the only one who can access your encryption key to your data. This means that if you forget your password, the software company cannot help you retrieve it. Lastly, it is important to know where the data center that will be holding your data is located. For example, if you are in Canada, your jurisdiction may prohibit you from holding client materials on a server located in the United States because of the Patriot Act and concerns over access by the National Security Agency (NSA).

In the following list, an asterisk next to a software name indicates it is *not Web- or cloud-based:*

AbacusLaw Gold*: accounting, trust accounting, general ledger, time, billing

Abacus Private Cloud: trust accounting, general ledger, time, billing

Actionstep: trust accounting, time, billing

Amicus Cloud: trust accounting, time, billing

Amicus Small Firm Accounting*: trust accounting, accounting, time, billing

Bill4Time: trust accounting, time, billing

Clio: trust accounting, time, billing

CosmoLex: trust accounting, accounting, general ledger, time, billing

Credenza Pro*: trust accounting, time, billing

Firm Central: trust accounting, time, billing

HoudiniESQ: trust accounting, time, billing

Leap: trust accounting, time, billing

MyCase: trust accounting, time, billing

PCLaw*: trust accounting, time, billing

ProLaw*: accounting, time, billing

RocketMatter: trust accounting, accounting, time, billing

Sage Timeslips*: trust accounting, time, billing

Tabs3 Billing*: trust accounting, accounting, time, billing

Time and Billing: trust accounting, time, billing

TimeSolv Legal: trust accounting, time, billing

TurboLaw Time and Billing* & Cloud: trust accounting, time, billing

Zola Suite: trust accounting, accounting, time, billing

Again, the cost of accounting software is so reasonable that there is no reason that a law firm should be keeping track of transactions manually. In these software applications, entry making is so easy that most programs automatically debit or credit the cash account when a check or deposit is recorded. As already stated, dual-entry bookkeeping is built into your program, and you just need to ensure that all transactions are recorded promptly and adequate reports to track the funds for each client subaccount are set up.

QuickBooks for Trust Accounting

QuickBooks is the number one program recommended by accountants. In Canada, if you elect to use QuickBooks, be sure to use the Canadian version. It is relatively inexpensive for an accounting program, popular enough that there are usually support staff and bookkeepers who are familiar with it, relatively easy to learn, and—most important to the accountant—standardizes how the accountant's clients will be reporting their financial information for preparing the annual tax returns. In fact, QuickBooks provides an Accountant's Report that prepares and sends a read-only report to your accountant.

When first setting up QuickBooks, you can select *legal services* as your business type. This will place a lot of the correct legal industry category names in your chart of accounts.

As previously explained, although your trust account is a bank account that you designate as *Bank Account (CASH)—CLIENT TRUST ACCOUNT*, it is NOT an asset of your law firm. The money belongs to your clients or to other third parties. Therefore, the proper account category for all trust accounts is *Other Current Liability* because it is really money that you OWE to other people should they terminate their client relationship and demand a refund of money you have not yet earned.

You will find it easy to keep track of the money belonging to your clients and other third parties because under the category *Other Current Liability—CLIENT TRUST ACCOUNT*, you will set up individual Client Subaccounts, one for each named client: Subaccount Client A, Subaccount Client B, Subaccount Client C, and so forth (see Lesson 5).

It is interesting to note that once you enter transactions into your accounting software program, your chart of accounts will reflect the current balances in these accounts. In the following example, we see what the *Other Current Liabilities* would look like in your chart of accounts. Should you print a balance sheet from your program's report menu, you will see that the balance sheet includes the category *Other Current Liabilities*.

Here is how this looks in the chart of accounts:

Other Current Liabilities	$175,455
—CLIENT TRUST ACCOUNT	10,000
—Client A	3,000
—Client B	4,000
—Client C	3,000
—INCOME TAX PAYABLE	65,455
—PAYROLL TAXES PAYABLE	28,000
—SALARIES AND WAGES PAYABLE	72,000

This is how it looks in the balance sheet:

OTHER CURRENT LIABILITIES	
—CLIENT TRUST ACCOUNT	10,000
—INCOME TAX PAYABLE	65,455
—PAYROLL TAXES PAYABLE	28,000
—SALARIES AND WAGES PAYABLE	72,000
Total Other Current Liabilities	$175,455

As these examples show, you may have a number of Other Current Liabilities, such as CLIENT TRUST ACCOUNT, INCOME TAX PAYABLE, PAYROLL TAXES PAYABLE, and SALARIES AND WAGES PAYABLE.

Notice that the CLIENT TRUST ACCOUNT under Other Current Liabilities equals the sum of the Subaccounts for Client A, Client B, and Client C.

Your *Bank Account (CASH)—GENERAL OPERATING ACCOUNT* is an asset of your law firm. The money belongs to your law firm. Therefore, the proper account category for your General Operating Account is *Asset*.

As you enter transactions into your accounting software program, your chart of accounts will reflect the current balances in these accounts:

Assets	$81,000
—Cash	30,758
—General Operating Account	25,758
—Savings Account	5,000
—Accounts Receivable	7,042
—Supplies	1,200
—Furniture	12,000
—Equipment	18,000
—Accumulated Depreciation	(3,000)
—Prepaid Insurance	15,000

How does this look in the balance sheet?

ASSETS	
Current assets	
Cash	$ 30,758
Accounts receivable net	7,042
Supplies	1,200
Prepaid insurance	15,000
Total current assets	54,000
Property, furniture & equipment	
Furniture (net depreciation)	12,000
Equipment (net depreciation)	18,000
Less: accumulated depreciation	(3,000)
Total property, furniture, and equipment	27,000
Total assets	$ 81,000

Practice Tip: *Although accounting principles pertaining to trust accounts are generally consistent, you should check with your jurisdiction for any specific requirement pertaining to the proper setup of a chart of accounts.*

Be sure to check your accounting software program for whether transactions can be changed once entered without creating an audit trail of changes. In Peachtree, you would need to create special journal entries documenting any changes, while this is not the case in QuickBooks. Figures entered QuickBooks are easy to change and preserve no audit trail of these changes. For example, you can delete a transaction, and other than the popup window asking whether you are sure you want to delete the transaction and it cannot be reversed, that is it. The transaction vanishes with no record of its earlier existence or removal. This can be important for the reasons set out in the section "Preserve an Audit Trail" later in this lesson. So be careful to monitor what is done in QuickBooks. Just as some lawyers have a two-person system of opening mail and recording deposits, you may want to adopt a two-person system of entering QuickBook entries. Be careful to monitor your bank records, your transaction records, and your QuickBook entries.

Whether to Use Excel

There is no rule that requires you to use trust accounting software or software of any kind. You are responsible for properly managing your client trust account so that you know or can easily ascertain how much money you hold in your trust account at any given time and to whom it belongs, when and for how much the original deposits were made, whether any additional funds have been deposited and when, and when and for what purpose withdrawals were made.

While you could use Excel, you are well advised not to. Your practice certificate in Canada or law license in the United States is too precious to put at risk. A big part of protecting it requires keeping your financial books and records in pristine shape and under your regulator or regulatory agency. Lawyers are typically not trained in bookkeeping, and Excel lacks the audit trail that is the hallmark of professional accounting systems and that preserves all information entered into the system. Entries in Excel can be quickly changed with a minimum of keystrokes; there is no record kept of the original information. If you make a mistake in Excel, it may be difficult or impossible to go back and try to correct that error without creating more problems. You need to be careful when you are responsible for other people's money.

Excel is a valuable program for entering numbers together in a column and row chart format to organize data into understandable reports, and it includes the ability to perform calculations with this information by setting up mathematical formulas such as addition, subtraction, multiplication, or division. You usually don't include much written description beyond column headings and brief descriptions such as "source" and "purpose." You will just want more than a spreadsheet for trust accounting.

Preserving an Audit Trail

An audit trail allows you or your accountant or forensic auditor to follow all transactions in your financial accounts. This is important for detecting if there has been any embezzlement. Typically, an embezzler goes in and alters transactions to cover up theft. When it comes to your trust account, it is critical for you to protect the money because it belongs to clients and third parties. By preserving an audit trail, you will likely feel more confident should your bar regulatory agency conduct a random audit of your trust account. For example, the Washington State Bar Association conducts random audits of client trust accounts that frequently turn up inactive client accounts and outstanding checks, failure to properly reconcile accounts, and improper processing of overpayments made by clients. For a helpful article, go to http://www.wsba.org/~/media/Files/Licensing_Lawyer%20Conduct/IOLTA/helpimbeingauditedmarch2010barnews.ashx.

Audit trails are preserved in more sophisticated accounting programs such as Sage 50 Accounting, formerly known as Peachtree, which is a General Ledger accounting program that is used by some financial institutions that have plenty of checks and balances in place with multiple staff performing various accounting duties and other staff responsible for checking and verifying transactions.

How can you preserve an audit trail absent something built into a program? Print out reports and journals and have the staff person who prepared them initial them. Have a different person check and verify the transactions, and initial that this was done. Keep copies of all vender bills, and when the bill is paid, put the date paid and check number on the face of the bill along with the initials of who did so. Keep a copy of all vendor bills so notated with the monthly statement on which the check cleared the bank.

When the bank statement is reconciled and the three-way reconciliation is completed, have the staff member who did this date and initial the bank statement and reconciliation form. Have a separate person check and date and initial doing so.

Consider having an accountant perform an audit of your trust account records annually. If you have your tax return done by an accountant, you could easily provide these records to be reviewed in an annual audit. Have the accountant provide a statement that an audit of the client trust account has been completed with his or her bill.

Doublechecking Entries

The biggest source of errors in trust accounting is mistakes in entries. You wrote down the wrong amount. You credited a deposit to the wrong client subaccount. You debited the wrong client subaccount. You paid the same vendor twice. If you are not using a program for trust accounting, you may have made a mathematical error.

You are only human. Errors happen. But if you check your entries, you will make fewer errors or catch them immediately and fix them. The longer there is an error, the greater the impact. The unfortunate reality of getting a notice of an overdraft in your trust account is discovering that you are stumped at finding out what went wrong. Frequently, the lawyer needs to go way back to find the error that started the problem.

Virtually all lawyers with the misfortune to overdraw their client trust account have a lot of room to improve their trust accounting system. It starts with checking all of your entries. This is a habit to cultivate so that it becomes second nature.

LESSON 7

Managing Your Trust Account

One Trust Account with Many Subaccounts

You will have an easier time managing your trust account if you think of it as one trust account with many subaccounts, one for each client or third party for whom you are holding money. You can't just deposit money into the trust account and write checks, estimating how much belongs to a specific individual. "They gave me $5,000 three months ago. I've only used about $500 for filing fees so there should be enough to cover my $1,000 bill for legal fees this month." You are not properly managing your trust account if you are merely guessing or estimating balances. You don't want to be on your way to being disciplined for mismanaging your trust account. To be sidelined from practicing law by a suspension for 30, 60, or 90 days may mean insolvency.

What Constitutes Proper Records

Consult your jurisdiction for specific requirements concerning how long your client trust account records need to be kept after a client matter is concluded. Be sure to check how long your bank preserves records of bank accounts before relying on your bank being able to supply you with electronic copies of your monthly statement. For example, in Oregon lawyers are required to keep their trust account records for five years after a client matter is closed. Most banks allow you to access bank account statements going back three years. Therefore, an Oregon attorney would need to preserve bank account statements as provided. By printing to a PDF, the attorney can keep the record in an electronic form that can be saved along with other client financial records.

In Canada, accounting records have to be kept for a minimum of ten years after a matter is closed, and in some cases even longer than that. Comment [1] to the ABA Model Rule 1.15 Safeguarding Property states, "A lawyer should maintain on a current basis books and records in accordance with generally accepted accounting practice and comply with any recordkeeping rules established by law or court order. See, e.g., Model Rules for Client Trust Account Records."

Your jurisdiction may not have adopted the ABA Model Rules for Client Trust Account Records. See Appendix C: ABA Model Rules for Client Trust Account Records. A review of Rule 1: Recordkeeping Generally with Comments will help you to understand what records could and should be kept for each client trust account you maintain. Here is a brief summary of the recommended records. These records can easily be printed from your trust accounting software. Prior to the use of software, they were prepared by hand.

1. Receipt and disbursement journals showing date, source, and description of deposits and date, payee, and purpose of disbursements
2. Client ledger records for all client subaccounts in your client trust account, showing, for each client, client's name, source, amount and description of deposited funds, description and amount of charges and withdrawals, and names of all recipients of funds disbursed

3. Copy of your retainer and fee agreement for each client
4. Copy of your accountings to each client showing all disbursements of funds
5. Copy of bills for legal fees and costs given to each client
6. Copy of records showing disbursements on behalf of each client
7. Physical or electronic equivalent of checkbook register, bank statements, records of deposits, prenumbered canceled checks, and substitute check items from your financial institution
8. Records of all electronic transfers from the client trust account, including name of who authorized the transfer, the date of the transfer, name of recipient, and confirmation from the financial institution of transfer, including date and time of transfer
9. Copy of monthly trial balance and quarterly reconciliation of client trust accounts
10. Copy of that portion of client file reasonably related to client trust account transaction

Keeping Track of Each Client's Money

Although you have opened one client trust account, you need to maintain ongoing accurate records of the sums you have deposited for each client. The way to do this is to set up a client ledger for each client on which you will track all funds for that client. In an accounting program, you will essentially set up a client ledger by creating a client subaccount for each client under the Client Trust Account.

If you are using a legal-specific trust accounting program, you will follow the directions to set up proper accounting for each client. Many small firms use QuickBooks for managing their firm's financial records. Although this software program is not legal-specific, you can set it up to provide proper accounting records for your overall client trust account and for each of the clients for whom you hold money in your client trust account. The client trust account is categorized as an Other Current Liability.

Your first transaction for a client is the opening deposit, usually a payment in advance of estimated legal fees or costs, or both. You will track all withdrawals from and deposits to the individual client subaccount until the work is completed, all of the funds are disbursed, and the subaccount for the particular client is reduced to a zero balance.

Accuracy requires that you do this accounting at the time you write checks and make deposits. By not waiting to record transactions, you will have an easier time keeping track of each client's money.

Client Ledger or Client Transaction Report

Prior to the use of accounting programs for computers, law firms tracked the funds for individual clients on a client ledger card, which was a form on buff color cardstock that allowed easy tracking of each client's money, all deposits, and all withdrawals. Many jurisdictions still refer to a client "ledger card" even though law firms are using accounting software to manage their client trust account. Essentially a client ledger card shows all transactions for a client, commencing from the first money given to the lawyer in advance of being earned as legal fees and in advance of any legal costs that are paid up front before the costs are incurred. You can think of this as analogous to an opening deposit. As you perform legal work and bill against the client trust funds according to the terms of your fee agreement, you will record the important information, date, amount, check number, purpose, recipient, and the balance of the client trust funds. Similarly, if you pay for legal costs, you will record the important information. Should you receive further deposits from the client or from some other source, such as a settlement, you would record the important information regarding the deposit date, amount, check number, purpose, issuer, and the balance of the client trust funds.

Your accounting program will allow you to compose various reports. A very basic common report is a transaction report. All reports allow you to specify the report period of time. To report all transactions to date for a client, begin with the date of the opening deposit and end with the date you want for the ending balance. If you are providing monthly reports, it makes sense to select the beginning date and ending date to correspond to the beginning and end of the month. If you want to provide a printout of the month's transactions, the start date would be the beginning of the month and the end date would be the end of the month.

You might want to provide this report of the entire month's transactions with your monthly statement for your client or copy it into a monthly statement format to report transactions in the client's trust account along with a detailed billing statement showing time spent on the matter and legal costs. Otherwise, the client will only see a line item in the client trust account transaction report indicating a payment was made for legal services.

You will easily be able to set up a monthly transaction report that can be run for each client subaccount that gets saved as a special report so that all you need to do is select the report type, the client, and the start and end date. This client transaction report will help you to accurately reconcile your trust account, typically monthly, when you receive your bank statement for your client trust account.

Tracking an individual client this way makes it clear how much money you hold for the client and whether there are adequate funds on deposit before you write a trust account check to pay for costs on behalf of the client.

Illustration 7.1 Client Ledger or Transaction Report for Alan Anderson

				CLIENT COSTS ADVANCED			FEES FOR LEGAL SERVICES			CLIENT TRUST ACCOUNT		
Date	Name	Memo	Ck. No.	Costs Advanced	Costs Received	Costs Balance	Fees Charged	Fees Received	AR Balance	Trust Funds Received	Trust Funds Disbursed	Trust Account Balance
BALANCE FORWARD												0
9/1/16	Alan Anderson	Retainer rec'd	Client Ck. #1564			0			0	$5,000		$5,000
9/7/16	Linn County Court	Client A's court filing fee		$150		$150			0			$5,000
9/30/16	Law Firm	Billed costs advanced				$150			0			$5,000
9/30/16	Law Firm	Billed legal fees				$150	$500		$500			$5,000
9/30/16	Alan Anderson	Costs from retainer	Trust Acct. Ck. #1010			$150			$500		$150	$4,850
9/30/16	Law Firm	Costs reimbursed			$150	0			$500			$4,850
9/30/16	Alan Anderson	Fees from retainer	Trust Acct. Ck. #1011			0			$500		$500	$4,350
9/30/16	Law Firm	Fees applied to AR				0		$500	0			$4,350
10/30/16	Law Firm	Billed legal fees				0	$1,000		$1,000			$4,350
10/30/16	Alan Anderson	Fees from retainer	Trust Acct. Ck. #1015			0			$1,000		$1,000	$3,350
10/30/16	Law Firm	Fees applied to AR				0		$1,000	0			$3,350

				CLIENT COSTS ADVANCED			FEES FOR LEGAL SERVICES			CLIENT TRUST ACCOUNT		
Date	Name	Memo	Ck. No.	Costs Advanced	Costs Received	Costs Balance	Fees Charged	Fees Received	AR Balance	Trust Funds Received	Trust Funds Disbursed	Trust Account Balance
11/2/16	Expert Witness Fees	Client A's EW fees	Operating Account Ck. #2500	$2,000		$2,000			0			$3,350
11/30/16	Law Firm	Billed costs advanced				$2,000			0			$3,350
11/30/16	Law Firm	Billed legal fees				$2,000	$1,350		$1,350			$3,350
11/30/16	Alan Anderson	Costs from retainer	Trust Acct. Ck. #1018			$2,000			$1,350		$2,000	$1,350
11/30/16	Law Firm	Costs reimbursed			$2,000	0			$1,350			$1,350
11/30/16	Alan Anderson	Fees from retainer	Trust Acct. Ck. #1019									
						0			$1,350		$1,350	0
11/30/16	Law Firm	Fees applied to AR				0		$1,350	0			0

A Glimpse of a New Firm

New Law Firm has had a busy first month and acquired four new clients Alan Anderson, Betty Brady, Cathy Calhoun, and Douglas Davis. Let's see how these accounting concepts work for tracking their financial records.

You need to set up subaccounts for each person with money in your trust account and keep proper records; otherwise you will find it impossible to manage your trust account and impossible to provide accurate reports to your clients. For example, suppose your bank records that on September 1, 2016, you have established a new trust account with an opening deposit of $5,000 representing a retainer for an employment law matter for new client Alan Anderson. You set up a subaccount to track the Anderson trust account. On September 5, 2016, you deposit $10,000 representing a retainer for a land use matter for new client Betty Brady. You set up a subaccount to track the Brady trust account. On September 6, 2016, you deposit $3,200 representing a retainer for estate planning for new client Cathy Calhoon. You set up a subaccount to track the Calhoon trust account. On September 15, 2016, you deposit $7,500 representing a retainer for a civil litigation matter for new client Douglas Davis. You set up a subaccount to track the Davis trust account. Essentially, you are acting as a bank for these four clients and will need to carefully monitor how much money you hold for each of them by entering their respective transactions in their subaccounts. In accordance with your fee agreement, you withdraw money from the trust account for reimbursement of costs advanced and payments of legal fees earned.

Before writing any trust account checks on behalf of a client, be careful to wait until newly deposited funds are collected as opposed to being cleared; otherwise you may be using money belonging to a different client. For example, on Thursday, September 15, 2016, Alan

Anderson's trust account balance is $5,000, Betty Brady's trust account balance is $10,000, and Cathy Calhoon's trust account balance is $3,200. Douglas Davis retains your legal services for civil litigation and gives you a retainer for $7,500. On Friday, September 16, 2016, you file the civil law suit for Douglas Davis and use your firm's credit card for paying the eCourt filing fee of $250, which is an advanced cost for which you will reimburse the firm from the Davis retainer at the end of the month.

On Monday, September 19, 2016, the lawyer receives a $1,500 invoice from the land surveyor in the Betty Brady case, and $75 invoice for the process server in the Douglas Davis case. The law firm pays these two invoices with the law firm general operating account, which are both advanced costs for which you will reimburse the firm from the Brady and Davis retainers at the end of the month. You would likely want to wait to reimburse the firm for advanced client costs at the same time you withdraw your legal fees. However, your retainer agreement may allow you to pay costs as they are incurred. If you directly paid the $75 process server's invoice for Davis with a trust account check on Monday, September 19, 2016, you very likely would have used money belonging to your other clients because it is doubtful that the Davis retainer check for $7,500 you deposited on Thursday, September 15, 2016, would be collected from the bank on which Davis wrote his retainer check.

The collected funds in your trust account on September 19, 2016, is actually $18,200, which would cover writing trust account checks to pay the two invoices, $1,500 for the Brady survey, and $75 for the Davis process server. The trust account would not be overdrawn. The bank would not be aware that you had improperly used trust account funds belonging to Anderson, Brady, and Calhoon to cover the $75 process server fee on behalf of Davis. Since your trust account is not overdrawn, the bank would not notify your jurisdiction's regulatory division that you had overdrawn your trust account. Your mistake here would be to rely on what the computer program showed as the Davis subaccount balance and not to verify that the funds were actually collected from the Davis checking account and in your client trust account before writing the $75 process service check on September 19, 2016.

This is how lawyers get into unfortunate situations with their trust account, as there could have been an overdraft created by writing checks against uncollected trust account funds. Always wait an adequate period of time after depositing a check for it to be collected from the bank account on which it is drawn. Your accounting program may allow you to flag transactions and/or attach a note. Consider flagging and/or notating a deposit transaction to indicate the date that the funds will be collected and available. If allowed in your jurisdiction, a wire transfer of funds to the client trust account would be available upon completion of the transfer. You cannot put a stop payment on a wire transfer, so if you have received one, it is in your account and the wire-transferred amount is available.

Practice Tip: *Be sure to ask your bank when funds are collected. Check with your jurisdiction for a reasonable amount of time to wait for a deposited amount to become available. When developing your law firm's policy, consider the time periods necessary for local, in-state, and out-of-state issuing banks. If allowed in your jurisdiction, consider the use of wire transfers, in which case the funds are available upon completion of the wire transfer.*

Wrap Up of First Month Ending September 30, 2016

New law firm has done well for its first month of business. At the end of the month, September 30, 2016, Law Firm sends out the following statements reflecting legal fees reimbursements to Law Firm for prepaid client costs.

Alan Anderson: retainer paid $5,000, reimbursement of court filing fee $150, legal fees $500, balance in trust account $4,350.

Betty Brady: retainer paid $10,000, reimbursement of land survey $1,500, legal fees $375, balance in trust account $8,125.

Cathy Calhoun: retainer paid $3,200, legal fees $3,000, refund of remaining trust account funds to client $200, balance in trust account $0.

Douglas Davis: retainer paid $7,500, reimbursement of court filing fee $250, reimbursement of process service $75, legal fees $450, refund of remaining trust account funds to client $6,725, balance in trust account $0.

At the end of the month, you run a trial balance after deducting these costs and fees. The trial balance shows how much money is held on September 30, 2016:

LAW OFFICE TRIAL BALANCE

September 30, 2016

CLIENT TRUST ACCOUNT BALANCES

Anderson, Alan	4,350
Brady, Betty	8,125
Calhoon, Cathy	0
Davis, Douglas	0
Total Client Trust Account Balances	$12,475

Although lawyers may track their client trust account in their QuickBooks program, many times they have not properly set up individual subaccounts for each client; thus it is understandable that they have lost track of how much money is held for each client.

Each client will be set up and treated as a subaccount of the client trust account. Check your chart of accounts to be sure that all client subaccounts correctly reflect their respective balance held in your client trust account. The Bank Account for the Client Trust Account should equal the Client Trust Account under Current Liabilities. See the following example showing balances at the end of their first month, September, 30, 2016:

Bank Account: General Operating Account			26,325		
Bank Account: Client Trust Account			12,475		
Other Current Liabilities			177,930		
	Client Trust Account			12,475	
		Anderson, Alan			4,350
		Brady, Betty			8,125
		Calhoon, Cathy			0
		Davis, Douglas			0
	Income Tax Payable			65,455	
	Payroll Taxes Payable			28,000	
	Salaries and Wages Payable			72,000	

Let's look at a Client Ledger Card or Transaction Report and see how it reflects the transactions made in the client's trust account. Client Alan Anderson, hires Law Firm to provide legal services. Their fee agreement requires him to pay a $5,000 deposit to cover future legal fees and costs.

1. On September 1, 2016, Alan Anderson gives Law Firm check number 1564 in the amount of $5,000 as a retainer for future legal costs and fees. In the accounting program, Law Firm records the date, name, memo detail, and check number of the $5,000 unearned fees and costs. This deposit is recorded in the *Bank Account (CASH)—CLIENT TRUST ACCOUNT* as "Trust Funds Received" and in *Other Current Liabilities—CLIENT TRUST ACCOUNT,* Subaccount for Anderson. (Note: Law Firm would set up a new subaccount for Alan Anderson if it has not already been created, which is easily done by selecting "Create New Subaccount" on the menu for any of the accounts you wish to track income and expenditures for, specifically for Alan Anderson, for example, in *Other Current Liabilities—CLIENT TRUST ACCOUNT, Advanced Costs*, and *Accounts Receivable.*) Alan Anderson's trust account balance is now $5,000 shown in *Other Current Liabilities—CLIENT TRUST ACCOUNT, Subaccount Alan Anderson.* The $5,000 retainer check from Alan Anderson is a deposit to Law Firm's bank account designated Client Trust Account. This $5,000 is a current liability owed to Alan Anderson, meaning that it would need to be repaid to Alan Anderson if he terminated services before the law firm had earned fees or expended clients' costs on his behalf.
2. On September 7, 2016, Law Firm electronically files Client Anderson's employment law case in the Linn County Court and pays the $150 eCourt filing fee with Law Firm's credit card. This is considered an advanced cost. In the accounting program, Law Firm records the date, name, and memo detail of the $150 eCourt filing fee as a "Credit Card Charge" and records this transaction as a "Client Costs Advanced" for Alan

Anderson by selecting (or creating) a subaccount under Client Costs Advanced for Alan Anderson. The subaccount for Alan Anderson's cost balance is $150.

3. On September 30, 2016, Law Firm bills for costs advanced in the amount of $150 and legal fees in the amount of $500. Because Law Firm's fee agreement states that fees and costs will be paid from the retainer provided by Alan Anderson, Law Firm is billing against Alan Anderson's retainer. Law Firm sends a statement to Alan Anderson detailing these transactions during the month of September, and showing his month-end balance of $4,350 in the trust account. In the accounting program, Law Firm records the date, name, and memo detail of the $500 legal fees billed as "Fees for Legal Services" and records this under Accounts Receivable Subaccount Alan Anderson. The subaccount for Alan Anderson's accounts receivable balance is $500. Note that the $150 advanced client costs was recorded earlier on September 7, 2016, as CLIENT COSTS ADVANCED: Costs Advance; therefore, his CLIENT COSTS ADVANCED: Costs Balance remains $150.
4. Also on September 30, Law Firm writes check number 1010 from the Trust Account, payable to Law Firm, in the amount of $150 to reimburse Law Firm for Alan Anderson's advanced client costs. In the accounting program, Law Firm records the date, name, and memo detail of the $150 disbursement to Law Firm on behalf of Alan Anderson from *Bank Account (CASH)—CLIENT TRUST ACCOUNT* and in *Other Current Liabilities—CLIENT TRUST ACCOUNT*, selects the subaccount Alan Anderson to record *Trust Funds Disbursed*. Alan Anderson's trust account balance is now reduced $150

to a balance of $4,850. Law Firm records the receipt of the reimbursement of advanced client costs as *CLIENT COSTS ADVANCED: Costs Received*. Alan Anderson's *CLIENT COSTS ADVANCED: Costs Balance* is now decreased $150 to a balance of $0.

5. Also on September 30, Law Firm writes check number 1011 from the client trust account payable to Law Firm in the amount of $500 for Alan Anderson's legal fees. Typically, a lawyer writes one check from the client trust account covering both the repayment of advanced costs and legal fees, but to make it easier to follow all transactions in the trust account, Law Firm has chosen to write two separate checks drawn against the funds held on behalf of Alan Anderson to reimburse the firm for advanced client costs and to pay legal fees earned and now payable. In the accounting program, Law Firm records the date, name, memo detail, and check number of the $500 disbursement from *Bank Account (CASH)—Client Trust Account* as "trust funds disbursed" for Alan Anderson. Law Firm records this disbursement in *Other Current Liability—CLIENT TRUST ACCOUNT, Subaccount Alan Anderson* for legal fees, and Alan Anderson's trust account balance is now reduced $500 to a balance of $4,350. Law Firm then records the receipt of the $500 fees as *FEES FOR LEGAL SERVICES: Fees Received* under Accounts Receivable for subaccount Alan Anderson. The subaccount for Alan Anderson's accounts receivable balance has been decreased $500 to a balance of $0.
6. On October 30, 2016, Law Firm bills for legal fees in the amount of $1,000 against Alan Anderson's retainer. Law Firm sends a statement to Alan Anderson detailing all transactions during the month of October. In the accounting program,

Law Firm notates the date, name, and memo detail of the $1,000 legal fees billed as *FEES FOR LEGAL SERVICES, Fees Charged* under Accounts Receivable Subaccount for Alan Anderson. The subaccount for Alan Anderson's accounts receivable balance is increased to $1,000.

7. Also on October 30, 2016, Law Firm writes check number 1015 from the client trust account payable to Law Firm in the amount of $1,000 for Alan Anderson's legal fees. In the accounting program, Law Firm records the date, name, memo detail, and check number of the disbursement to Law Firm from *Bank Account (CASH)—CLIENT TRUST ACCOUNT* as trust funds disbursed for Alan Anderson. Law Firm records this disbursement in *Other Current Liability—CLIENT TRUST ACCOUNT,* Subaccount Alan Anderson for legal fees, and Alan Anderson's *Trust Account Balance* is now reduced $1,000 to a balance of $3,350. Law Firm records the receipt of the $1,000 legal fees from Alan Anderson as *FEES FOR LEGAL SERVICES: Fees Received* under Accounts Receivable subaccount for Alan Anderson. The subaccount for Alan Anderson's accounts receivable balance is reduced from $1,000 to a balance of $0.
8. On November 2, 2016, Law Firm writes a check number 2500 from Law Firm's Operating Account payable to Dr. Robert Kline, the expert witness in Alan Anderson's case, in the amount of $2,000 for Alan Anderson's advanced costs. (Note: Because Law Firm is paying the fees by check, Law Firm could have written a check for $2,000 directly from the client trust account as Alan Anderson had sufficient money in the client trust account. Instead, Law Firm had chosen to limit the use of the trust account checks solely to be used for payments to the

law firm or payments directly to the client. Law Firm adopted this policy after an embezzlement that happened to another law firm made Law Firm fear that having a greater number of trust account checks floating around bearing the trust account number and bank routing number is how law firm trust accounts can be accessed by fraudsters. In the accounting program, Law Firm records the date, name, memo detail, and check number of the $2,000 expert witness fee in *Bank Account (CASH) General Operating* as client costs advanced and records this advanced client cost in *CLIENT COSTS ADVANCED: Costs Advanced*, subaccount for Alan Anderson, and his *CLIENT COSTS ADVANCED: Costs Balance* is now increased $2,000 to a balance of $2,000.

9. On November 30, 2016, Law Firm bills for costs advanced in the amount of $2,000 and legal fees in the amount of $1,350 against Alan Anderson's retainer. Law Firm sends him a statement detailing all transactions during the month of November. In the accounting program, Law Firm records the date, name, and memo detail of the $1,350 legal fees billed as FEES FOR LEGAL SERVICES: Fees Charged under the Accounts Receivable subaccount for Alan Anderson. FEES FOR LEGAL SERVICES: Accounts Receivable, the subaccount for Alan Anderson's accounts receivable balance, is increased to $1,350.
10. Also on November 30, 2016, Law Firm writes check number 1018 from the client trust account payable to Law Firm in the amount of $2,000 for reimbursing Law Firm for Alan Anderson's advanced client costs. In the accounting program, Law Firm records the date, name, memo detail, and check number of the $2,000 disbursement to Law Firm from Bank Account (CASH)—CLIENT TRUST ACCOUNT as trust

funds disbursed for Alan Anderson. Law Firm records this disbursement in Other Current Liability—CLIENT TRUST ACCOUNT, subaccount Alan Anderson Trust Funds Disbursed. Alan Anderson's trust balance is reduced $2,000 to a balance of $1,350. Law Firm records the receipt of the reimbursed advanced client costs in CLIENT COSTS ADVANCED: Costs Advanced for Alan Anderson's client costs subaccount, and his CLIENT COSTS ADVANCED: Costs Balance is reduced $2,000 to a balance of $0.

11. Also on November 30, 2016, Law Firm writes check number 1019 from the client trust account payable to Law Firm in the amount of $1,350 for Alan Anderson's legal fees. Law Firm notates the date, name, memo detail, and check number and records the disbursement of $1,350 to Law Firm from Bank Account (CASH)—CLIENT TRUST ACCOUNT as trust funds disbursed from Alan Anderson. Law Firm records this disbursement in Other Current Liability—CLIENT TRUST ACCOUNT, subaccount Alan Anderson, and his trust balance is reduced $1,350 to a balance of $0. Law Firm notates the receipt of the $1,350 fees as FEES FOR LEGAL SERVICES: Fees Received under the Accounts Receivable subaccount for Alan Anderson, and his FEES FOR LEGAL SERVICES: Accounts Receivable Balance becomes reduced $1,350 to a balance of $0.
12. At the conclusion of November 30, 2016, on the Client Ledger Card or Transaction Report for Alan Anderson, these are his balances: *CLIENT COSTS ADVANCED: Costs Balance* is $0; *FEES FOR LEGAL SERVICES: Accounts Receivable Balance* is $0; and *CLIENT TRUST ACCOUNT: Trust Account Balance* is $0. If Law Firm has further work to do for Alan Anderson in this matter, Law Firm would either need to request

> a replenishment of a retainer or advanced costs and fees, or would need to bill the client monthly. It is always helpful to put a provision into a fee agreement to require a replenishment of the retainer. If a replenishment agreement has not been included in Law Firm's fee agreement with Alan Anderson, then Law Firm would need to bill Alan Anderson at the end of each month going forward until the matter is concluded.

Whether you are confidently using an electronic accounting system or carefully using a calculator or ten-key, the steps will be roughly similar. Once you have used an electronic accounting system, you will likely never want to return to paper, pencil, and calculator.

Technology is a tool that enables you to save time and improve accuracy. There is no need to struggle to keep track of your individual clients by setting up individual subaccounts on physical client ledger cards and updating each of these by hand. It is much easier, more cost-effective, and even likely to be more accurate to set up your client subaccounts in your accounting software program. A transaction report for each client subaccount in the *Other Current Clients—CLIENT TRUST ACCOUNT* will pull all of the information traditionally included on a physical client ledger card, enabling you to track disbursements and deposits to each client's trust account. Print these out for reconciling your client trust and providing reports to your client.

Your bar association may refer to the process of "keeping client ledger cards." If you are required to keep these in a paper format, print out and keep a monthly transaction report for each client who has money in your client trust account. Your bar may have a sample to guide you in customizing the client transaction report to provide the same records. Technology makes this easy.

The Trust Account Journal or Transaction Register

The trust account journal is a form that replaces the checkbook register. Its full name is the "journal of receipts and disbursements." Some may use a separate journal of receipts and a journal of disbursements. It does not need to be paper unless your bar association requires you to maintain paper records. Some lawyers may find it best to use their No Carbon Required (NCR) or carbon paper double-copy receipt book as a receipts journal in which they record every payment received. If they receive a check, they destroy the top copy of the receipt, and the bottom copy remains in the receipt book so that adding up funds received is an easy process. Whether you are doing your recordkeeping in a checkbook register, receipts journal, or electronically in an accounting program, the trust account journal is the accounting form on which you track the overall deposits and withdrawals made in your client trust account. To preserve a record of your trust account journal when using an accounting program, print out a copy of the entire client trust account transaction register for the month, showing your opening and ending balance for the month plus all transactions.

The trust account journal or transaction register that Law Firm uses is fairly self-explanatory. Notice that it has two major sections to keep track of all incoming deposits to Law Firm's trust account and of all outgoing disbursements from Law Firm's trust account. You can see all the clients for whom Law Firm holds client trust account money: the four clients who paid retainers in September: Alan Anderson, Betty Brady, Cathy Calhoon, and Douglas Davis; and the seven clients who paid retainers in October: Edward Envers, Fiona Frank, Gary Galvin, Helen Hendrix, Ione Ingram, John Jones, and Karen Kenny. Each of them has a client ledger or a subaccount set up in the accounting program, which can be printed out as a client transaction report by selecting the proper client account in the reports section of the program. You can see that Alan Anderson is the first transaction in Law Firm's trust account journal.

In QuickBooks, you can record a transaction using journal entries or can use the checkbook, making a record as you write checks and make deposits.

Either way, be sure to properly allocate the deposit or withdrawal from the correct client subaccount. Do not record a transaction by the electronic checkbook, *Banking: Write Checks and Make Deposits,* and the account journal method; otherwise you are going to duplicate your transactions. Most lawyers and their bookkeeping staff are frequently more comfortable entering transactions by using the accounting program's checkbook feature, *Banking: Make Deposits and Write Checks*, because it mirrors what they are doing with their paper client trust account checkbook. If you don't want to have your program print out checks, you still can make out checks by hand. Note that managing transactions via the *Banking* feature will still allow you to print out trust account journals. Your program will pull all transactions into account journals because your program is a general ledger accounting program. An account journal captures transactions in each account established when you set up your chart of accounts. These are collectively known as journal entries.

It is a simple matter to set up reports in QuickBooks so that you can print out the transactions in your overall client trust account that will show the entire collection of deposits and withdrawals. This is the equivalent of a trust account journal. If you elect to pull a report just showing all deposits, this is the equivalent of a journal of receipts; a report just showing all disbursements is the equivalent of a journal of disbursements. Under the *Reports* feature of your accounting program, you will be able to select what accounts you want to see in a report and what details, and select the time period.

Illustration 7.2 Trust Account Journal or Transaction Register for Law Firm

		Deposits To Client Trust Account			Withdrawals from Client Trust Account				Trust Account Balance
Date	Check Number	Receipts Amount	Source	Description of Deposited Item	Check Number	Disbursements Amount	Payee	Purpose of Disbursement	Balance
9/1/16	Client Ck. #1564	$5,000	Anderson, Alan	Retainer for Employment Law					$5,000
9/5/16	Client Ck. #2221	$10,000	Brady, Betty	Retainer for Land Use					$15,000
9/6/16	Client Ck. #1201	$3,200	Calhoon, Cathy	Retainer for Estate Planning					$18,200
9/15/16	Client Ck. #3995	$7,500	Davis, Douglas	Retainer for Civil Litigation					$25,700
9/30/16					Trust Acct. Ck. #1001	$3,000	Law Firm	Calhoon, fees	$22,700
9/30/16					Trust Acct. Ck. #1002	$200	Cathy Calhoon	Calhoon, bal of trust funds	$22,500
9/30/16					Trust Acct. Ck. #1003	$1,500	Law Firm	Brady, adv. costs land survey	$21,000
9/30/16					Trust Acct. Ck. #1004	$375	Law Firm	Brady, fees	$20,625
9/30/16					Trust Acct, Ck. #1005	$250	Law Firm	Davis, adv. costs filing fee	$20,375
9/30/16					Trust Acct. Ck. #1006	$75	Speedy Server	Davis, process server	$20,300
9/30/16					Trust Acct. Ck. #1007	$450	Law Firm	Davis, fees	$19,850
9/30/16					Trust Acct. Ck. #1008	0	VOIDED	Voided ck written in error	$19,850
9/30/16					Trust Acct. Ck. #1009	$6,725	Douglas Davis	Davis, bal of trust funds	$13,125
9/30/16					Trust Acct. Ck. #1010	$150	Law Firm	Anderson, adv. costs filing	$12,975
9/30/16					Trust Acct. Ck. #1011	$500	Law Firm	Anderson, fees	$12,475
10/1/16	Client Ck. #2787	$5,000	Envers, Edward	Retainer for Dom Rel					$17,475

		Deposits To Client Trust Account			Withdrawals from Client Trust Account				Trust Account Balance
Date	Check Number	Receipts Amount	Source	Description of Deposited Item	Check Number	Disbursements Amount	Payee	Purpose of Disbursement	Balance
10/5/16	Client Ck. #1053	$2,500	Frank, Fiona	Retainer for Guardianship					$19,975
10/7/16	Client Ck. #2500	$7,500	Galvin, Gary	Retainer for Dom Rel					$27,475
10/7/16	Client Ck. #3445	$2,800	Hendrix, Helen	Retainer for Dom Rel					$30,275
10/9/16	Client Ck. #2019	$3,500	Ingram, Ione	Retainer for Dom Rel					$33,775
10/26/16	Client Ck. #3677	$3,000	Jones, John	Retainer for Estate Planning					$36,775
10/28/16	Client Ck. #2698	$2,500	Kenny, Karen	Retainer for Dom Rel					$39,275
10/30/16					Trust Acct. Ck. #1012	$180	Law Firm	Envers, adv. costs psych eval	$39,095
10/30/16					Trust Acct. Ck. #1013	$250	Law Firm	Envers, adv. costs filing fee	$38,845
10/30/16					Trust Acct. Ck. #1014	$800	Law Firm	Envers, Fees	$38,045
10/30/16					Trust Acct. Ck. #1015	$1,000	Law Firm	Anderson, Fees	$37,045
10/30/16					Trust Acct. Ck. #1016	$3,000	Law Firm	Jones, Fees	$34,045
10/30/16					Trust Acct. Ck. #1017	$1,000	Law Firm	Ingram, Fees	$33,045
11/30/15					Trust Acct. Ck. #1018	$2,000	Law Firm	Anderson, costs	$31,045
11/30/16					Trust Acct. Ck. #1019	$1,350	Law Firm	Anderson, Fees	$29,695
11/30/16					Trust Acct. Ck. #1020	$3,000	Law Firm	Jones, Fees	$26,695
11/30/16					Trust Acct. Ck. #1021	$5,000	Law Firm	Brady, Fees	$21,695

Form for Monthly Reconciliations

The checking account statement from the bank has an account reconciliation form on the back, and it's a great, easy way to understand the monthly reconciliation process. On it, you will reconcile the trust balance your internal records show to what the bank reports on the statement by adding any additional deposits that were not received by your bank and by subtracting any checks and withdrawals not received and processed by the bank by the statement cutoff date. This adjusted balance should now equal what your checkbook register or trust account journal shows, depending on how you track your overall balance in the trust account.

You will also want to reconcile the adjusted balance in the bank account to the sum of all your client ledgers plus any amount of your money you hold in the trust account for the sole purpose of paying bank fees. If doing the reconciliation by hand, you would use a trust account reconciliation form. It will allow you to add up the balances of all client ledgers, the balance of that month's reconciled bank statement, and then the balance shown in your checkbook register or trust account journal. If using trust accounting software, there will be a reconciliation feature that accomplishes what is just described. All three amounts should equal each other. This is known as a three-way reconciliation and is discussed in more detail in the next lesson. It is easy to set up a form that can be used for this three-way reconciliation or print out the form generated by your accounting software. It should be kept as part of your client trust accounting records.

LESSON 8

Balancing Your Trust Account

One of the most important duties related to your trust account is making sure that it remains in balance. Reconciling your records to the records kept by your bank verifies that all transactions have been recorded properly. Reconciling your trust account ensures that all receipts and disbursements were carried out as they were supposed to be. If you don't balance your account, you will not be managing your client trust account. How can you catch any errors if you do not balance your account? If you cannot determine to the penny how much money each client has in your client trust account, you are sure to make errors that will harm your clients and get you into trouble with your bar regulators for failing to properly protect the property belonging to clients and third parties.

How to Balance Your Trust Account

When your monthly trust account statement is received, gather together your checkbook register or trust account journal and your individual client ledger cards or equivalent reports for each subaccount.

If you are using an accounting program, you will be able to set up reports easily to give you the information that would be found in your paper checkbook register: all deposits, their date, their source and purpose, and all checks or withdrawals, their date, to whom issued and for what purpose. This report may be referred to as a "transaction register" or "account journal." All you have to do is indicate which account: Client Trust Account, and which date for the report start date and which date for the report end date.

In your accounting program, set up a report that allows you to print out all transactions for each client subaccount. Although you can have one report with each client reported as a subaccount, you may find it useful to also print out each subaccount separately. These separate reports can be kept as individual client trust account records. Remember that your duty to preserve confidentiality means that you would not want to disclose financial records that belong to another client or third person.

Your checking account statement from the bank has an account reconciliation form on the back. Confirm that the starting balance on the bank statement is accurate with your records. If this is the first time you have received your trust account statement, the opening account balance should be zero and the opening deposit will be the deposit with which you opened your trust account. Be sure that you have notated that the source of this deposit is your law firm's funds, if so. It is helpful to notate the source of your deposits on the bank statement and in your checkbook register or trust account journal.

Should you audit your trust account at a later date, having the source of deposits written onto the bank statement will make the audit process go more quickly because it will be easy to check the bank statement against the trust account journal and client ledger cards. You can accomplish this on your paper bank statement, or if you get an electronic statement, you can notate these details on the PDF. Your accounting program will have the source of deposits noted. Remember, the date of deposit or of withdrawal on the monthly statement will be the date the check was cleared or the deposit was credited by the bank; this is rarely the actual date you wrote the check or made the deposit. There is usually a delay of one or two banking days. If there are several deposits and or withdrawals for the same amount, look more closely at your records to determine which one. Some lawyers have gotten off track by not verifying to whom a check was written or from whom a deposit was received. You can't remember everything, but you can avoid forgetting anything if it has been properly recorded in detail in your accounting program or checkbook.

First, check off each deposit credited on the statement. If your trust account journal shows a deposit made but not credited, determine if it was made close to the bank statement date or later. Record these additional deposits on the back of the statement where your bank has provided a reconciliation form. The form will list them as "Outstanding Deposits" or something similar. Note that if you are reconciling your checking account in the accounting program, it will ask you to indicate the bank statement's closing balance, and then you will check all deposits received. Any unchecked deposits will be those not received by the bank by the bank statement's closing date.

If your records show that the missing deposit was made long enough before the statement cutoff date that it should have been received by the bank, follow up with the bank. You will want to show the bank your copy of your deposit slip with the items being deposited and the deposit receipt, if you were given one at the time of the deposit. (If you send someone to the bank to make your deposits for you, always insist that he or she returns the deposit receipt to you the same day or first thing the next morning. This will prevent staff members from forgetting to make deposits in a timely manner.) If the deposited item has been lost, let your client know soon so your client can put a stop payment on it and reissue the check.

Next, check off each cleared check on the statement. If your trust account journal shows that a check was written and sent or given to someone but has not cleared, determine if it was issued close to the bank statement date or later. Record these additional checks on the back of the statement. The form will list them as "Outstanding Checks" or something similar. Note that if you are reconciling your checking account in the accounting program, it will ask you to indicate the bank statement's closing balance, and then you will check all checks cleared. Any unchecked checks will be those not received by the bank by the bank statement's closing date.

Verify that any other debits (deductions from the account for bank fees or check printing) are shown in your records and are legitimate fees, charges, and withdrawals. Some financial institutions will add the IOLTA interest earned on the funds held in your trust account into the account and then deduct it and send it to the foundation. Others will simply note interest earned somewhere on the statement but will not add and deduct it to the account. It is unnecessary that you maintain a ledger for the IOLTA interest, as long as you check the statement to make sure that the same amount added to the account is deducted from the account in any month.

If you have a check that should have been cashed but was not, follow up. Otherwise, you are allowing client property to remain in your trust account past the time it should be paid out. This may happen because an expert witness or subpoenaed witness has not cashed his or her check for witness fees. If these checks are not eventually cashed, then at the end of representation you will need to return the money to your client. You don't want to end up with unclaimed client property in your client trust account.

Reconciling your client trust account bank statement is basically the same whether you do it on the paper statement or you use an accounting program. It is easy to do it with a program because the program lets you know that your banking statement is reconciled with your records.

Doing a Three-Way Reconciliation

Whether you are handling the accounting for the client trust account by hand or by use of a computer program, you will want to reconcile your overall client trust account transactions to the bank statement and to the total of your client subaccounts. First, create a Trial Balance by listing

Illustration 8.1 Three-way Reconciliation Statement for September 2016 for Law Firm

For the Month Ending September 30, 2016			
	CLIENT NAME	**CLIENT'S TRUST ACCOUNT BALANCE FROM CLIENT LEDGERS**	
	Anderson, Alan	$4,350.00	
	Brady, Betty	$8,125.00	
	Calhoon, Cathy	$0.00	
	Davis, Douglas	$0.00	
	LAW FIRM'S FUNDS FOR BANK CHARGES IF ANY	$0.00	
Section 1	**TOTAL FROM ALL CLIENT LEDGERS**		**$12,475.00**
Section 2	**TOTAL FROM TRUST ACCT JOURNAL TRANSACTION REGISTER**		**$12,475.00**
	BANK STATEMENT	$12,475.00	
	Less Outstanding Checks	$0.00	
	Plus In Transit Deposits	$0.00	
Section 3	**RECONCILED BANK STATEMENT BALANCE:**		**$12,475.00**

all subaccounts in the trust account and the amount in each, totaling this up. This Trial Balance total (from adding all of the client subaccounts, plus any amount of your law firm's money held to pay bank charges) should equal the checkbook register total or the trust account journal total and should also equal the reconciled bank statement total. That is a three-way reconciliation.

> **Practice Tip:** *A good bookkeeper who is familiar with legal accounting and your accounting system can easily save you a lot of headache, worry, and work and help you stay in compliance.*

Establishing Good Habits

Here are some good habits to follow:

1. The checking account statement from the bank should be opened and reviewed as soon as possible after receipt.
2. Set aside a date on your calendar for balancing your client trust account and general operating account. Do it on the date scheduled unless there is an emergency and you cannot devote enough time to do so.
3. Set aside a date on your calendar for sending out your billing statements on a monthly basis, and do so consistently.
4. Indicate a date on your billing statement and a due day for when you expect payment to be received if you are billing clients for services as work is completed instead of getting money up front.
5. If your clients owe you money, follow up by phone at 45 days to inquire why payment has not been received.
6. Your fee agreement should cover the expectation that your client pays your bills in a timely manner and that if bills are not

paid on time you will suspend work until the client's account is brought current.

7. Don't complain about not being paid, and continue to work.
8. Straighten out financial arrangements, such as by putting a payment plan into place, so that your client can cover the costs and legal fees agreed to in your fee agreement.
9. If the client is not paying your fees, assess if you need to withdraw from representation early enough so you won't be putting your client at a disadvantage.
10. Always review your rules of professional conduct, and if you have any questions, consult your bar's ethics counsel before withdrawing from representation.
11. On a quarterly basis, review your 12-month cash flow and make adjustments so you can meet your obligations and move toward a profitable law practice.
12. If you haven't prepared a business plan with a budget, it is never too late.

LESSON 9

Providing Reports to Clients and Third Parties

Imagine for a moment that you have been served with divorce papers and your spouse has taken off for parts unknown with your children. Feeling betrayed, upset, and angry, you go to a family law attorney who has been recommended to you by a co-worker. The lawyer seems to be everything one would want in a divorce attorney. You sign the engagement agreement and pay the $15,000 requested. You are told it will be placed into the lawyer's client trust account and that as legal fees and costs are incurred, the money will come from the $15,000. You are worried. You call the lawyer and are told not to worry, that the lawyer is hard at work on your case and will be in touch within a few days. Thirty days goes by. You call the lawyer again and leave your number. Well-meaning relatives begin to advise you. Another 30 days goes by. You wonder how much work has happened and how much of your money has been spent. Is any of it left? Should you call the state bar to file a complaint? You pick up the phone to call the lawyer one last time. He answers and you try to control your anger so at last you can find out what is going on.

I imagine you would not enjoy being that client, or that lawyer. Lawyers must communicate with their clients. But even common sense should guide lawyers in keeping their clients informed about their case, including what legal fees and costs are being incurred. If these are to be billed to the client's retainer or money is to be paid up front to cover legal fees and costs, the client should be advised on a timely ongoing basis. Since we are used to getting monthly statements for most of our expenses, it is expected that we would get a monthly statement from our lawyer.

What information should a statement provide? A client should be given a statement at the next statement time after paying advanced costs and fees or a retainer to the lawyer. This statement, just like a bank account statement, should show $0 balance carried forward and then show the date and amount of this initial retainer. If the engagement agreement calls for legal fees and costs to be paid from the retainer, you should provide an easy-to-understand itemized statement showing what legal services have been performed, the date performed, and if hourly billing then the amount of time spent and hourly rate, along with any legal costs incurred, including the date, description, and amount, and the balance remaining in the client's trust account. To provide a client with a statement that merely says, "$2,000 for legal services rendered" is not sufficient. It raises more questions than it answers.

In similar fashion, if you convey that an accepted settlement offer has been received, you should advise your client promptly. You should provide an accounting of the settlement payment so that the client will know how much was received, when, what costs of litigation were reimbursed to the firm, what medical liens were paid, how much the law firm collected for its share of the settlement proceeds based upon the signed contingency agreement, and how much the client receives. To provide a client with a settlement check and statement that merely says, "$52,000 for your share of the settlement proceeds" is not sufficient. It, too, raises more questions than it answers.

Both the ABA Model Rule 1.15 on Safekeeping Client Property and Federation of Law Societies of Canada's Federation Model Code

Illustration 9.1 Sample Monthly Statement to Client Alan Anderson for September 2016

Date	Description	Disbursed	Received	Balance in Client Trust Account
9/01/16	Balance fwd.			$0
9/01/16	Retainer paid		$5,000.00	$5,000.00
9/07/16	Prepare pleading to commence case 1.8 hrs. @ $200/hour: $360.00			
9/07/16	Advanced costs paid by Law Firm: filing fee for Linn county $150.00			
9/20/16	Telephone conf. w/opposing counsel 7 hrs. @$200/hour: $140.00			
9/30/16	Reimbursement of advanced costs: filing fee	$150.00		$4,850.00
9/30/16	Total legal services rendered 2.5 hrs. @ $200/hr. Robert Smith, Esq.	$500.00		$4,350.00

of Professional Conduct, Code 3.5: Preservation of Clients' Property require you to promptly notify your client or third party that you have received funds on their behalf. What does "promptly" mean? This term is not defined in the ethics rules, but it tends to be considered as what is reasonable under the circumstances. What is considered prompt notification may be dictated by the compelling nature of the case; for example, settling a huge medical malpractice wrongful death case may justify faster notification than a settlement in a minor fender bender, especially if the lawyer in tied up in a two-week capital murder trial.

Provide your client with a detailed itemization of the settlement proceeds under your contingency fee agreement when paying your client the client's share of settlement proceeds. Show what litigation costs were reimbursed to the law firm and what medical liens were paid, how much was paid to the law firm for the agreed-upon share, and how much is being paid to the client.

Practice Tip: *Be sure to keep up-to-date contact information for each client or other third party for whom you are holding property readily accessible so that you can provide statements of account or return their property.*

What Information to Provide

It is your client's money. Clients need to be given timely reports about their trust account funds. Any money received into your trust account that belongs in whole or in part to the client should be reported to the client.

Provide a receipt when your client first pays a retainer or pays a sum to cover anticipated costs and legal fees. Occasionally, your client may pay additional deposits to replenish his trust account balance, and provide a receipt and report these additional deposits in the monthly statement.

There may be settlement proceeds that are received, which initially must be deposited into your client trust account. Again, include the receipt of settlement proceeds into your client trust account to your client in the monthly statement.

When the settlement proceeds have been collected and are available for disbursement, provide your client with a separate settlement proceeds accounting to detail the amount received, the percentage of your law firm's contingency fee earned, the deduction for reimbursing the law firm for litigation costs that were incurred and paid by the law firm per your contingency fee agreement, any medical liens, and the balance paid to your client.

Throughout the time you hold funds in your trust account for your client, provide a monthly accounting of these funds or, at a minimum, during months for which there are transactions on behalf of the client. Substantiate all costs that you paid on the client's behalf, whether you paid them directly out of the trust account or you advanced the costs out of your general operating account and are now reimbursing your law firm from the client's funds held in the trust account.

It may be easiest to adopt a two-page monthly statement for your clients: page 1 detailing the legal services you provided and breakout of costs incurred, and page 2 providing an accounting of trust funds showing balance forward, deposits, costs paid or reimbursed to the law firm, payment of the total of legal fees owing from page 1, and the ending balance. Keep these records as part of your trust account records that must be kept for the length of time in your jurisdiction after a matter is closed.

Clients frequently forget that the costs incurred during litigation are to be reimbursed from their share of the settlement proceeds, not yours, if that is allowable in your jurisdiction. Then they are quite unhappy when they see you received your full 30 to 40 percent of the settlement proceeds but their 60 to 70 percent of the settlement shrank substantially after reimbursing your firm for the costs of litigation. They may feel you got the better deal and they got victimized again.

Avoid unhappy clients by keeping them properly informed. Unfulfilled unreasonable expectations lead to bar complaints.

What Details to Provide

Your client and third party need to know sufficient details about the funds being held in your trust account on their behalf. After first receiving funds on their behalf, provide a statement that shows a $0 balance forward and showing the date, amount, and reason that funds were received, such as "March 1, 2016, $5,000 retainer received from Client A, balance in client trust account $5,000." If you pay a cost directly from the retainer, you should provide a statement that shows the date, the payee, the purpose, and the amount of the check, such as "March 5,

2016, legal cost of $350 paid to Baker County Circuit Court for filing fee for case number FL15-4567, balance in client trust account $4,650." If you are reimbursing your law firm for payment of advanced costs, the date you advanced the cost and the purpose should be provided, such as "March 6, 2016, $350 to Law Firm for reimbursement paying advanced legal cost to Baker County Circuit Court for filing fee for case number FL15-4567, balance in client trust account $4,650." To be fully transparent, it is a good idea to provide a copy of the underlying charge for the costs paid in your report.

Provide sufficient detail to your client to support any legal fees paid. These can be itemized on a separate client billing statement and attached to the trust account statement, showing that the funds for the legal services have been deducted. The opening balance should be the same as the ending balance of the prior statement. Likewise, the ending balance on this statement will become the opening balance for the next reporting period.

How Often to Provide a Statement

Both the ABA Model Rules of Professional Conduct and the Federation Model Code of Professional Conduct require an attorney upon request to promptly render a full accounting regarding property in the attorney's possession. So, absent a request from the client, how often should you provide an accounting of the funds that you are holding?

Most clients will expect a monthly statement. At a minimum, provide a statement for any month in which a transaction affects your client's trust account balance and once per quarter otherwise. If you get in the habit of providing monthly statements, you will keep your clients informed and more satisfied with the level of communication. The same goes for reporting to any third party for whom you are holding funds.

If costs are mounting, your best approach is always to talk with your client promptly; otherwise you are setting the stage for an unhappy client not far down the road, one who is apt to file a bar complaint for either lack of communication or excessive fees and costs. It is considerate to call the client to give a heads-up before sending out a monthly statement that reports substantially increased costs or legal fees compared to earlier statements.

Combining Trust Account and Billing Statements

It is acceptable to provide a trust account statement that is combined with a billing statement. Just be clear in the design of your overall statement to set out information regarding the trust account. Here are four sections to include:

1. Current Legal Fees Section, a statement of your current time charges with enough detail so that your client will know what you did and when you did it and for how much;
2. Current Deposits to Trust Account Section, a statement itemizing any additional deposits the client has made to replenish the trust account or if any settlement proceeds have been deposited into the trust account on your client's behalf;
3. Current Costs Section, a statement itemizing any client costs; be sure to separate costs that the firm has paid on behalf of the client (Advanced Costs) and the costs that are paid directly from the client trust account (Direct Costs); and
4. Trust Accounting Section, a statement showing the opening balance in the client's trust account for this time period, any additional deposits received, the total of advanced costs being reimbursed to your firm, any costs being paid directly from the client's trust account, the amount of the legal fees being paid, and lastly, the ending balance in the client trust account.

LESSON 10

Closing Your Trust Account

At some point in the near or distant future, you will need to close your trust account. You may decide to transfer your banking to another bank that provides greater convenience or better service. You may decide to go into partnership with another lawyer and you need a trust account in the name of your new law firm. You may decide to close your solo practice to join a well-established firm that has its own trust account. You may become appointed judge or are no longer doing work that requires holding client funds. Or you may have decided that it is time to retire from the practice of law. In all of these situations, you will need to know how to properly close your client trust account.

Steps to Closing Your Trust Account

Step 1. Fully reconcile your trust account. Any funds remaining in the account should belong to specific clients or to your law firm if your jurisdiction had permitted you to hold a nominal amount of your money for the sole purpose of meeting minimum balance requirements or to cover reasonably anticipated bank charges.

Step 2. Contact your state bar association or provincial law society for specific instructions that your jurisdiction requires you to follow for closing your client trust account. In Canada, you would follow the directions of your law society in terms of closing down your trust account. Typically this would involve preparing and filing a final trust report in accordance with your law society's requirements. If your jurisdiction provides a practice management adviser, he or she can assist you with a checklist to help this process go smoothly. If there is no checklist, confirm that these steps provided here are appropriate for your jurisdiction.

Step 3. Determine whether your bank will assess any fee for closing your trust account. If the bank will impose a fee for closing the account, arrange for this fee to be taken from your general operating account, or you will need to deposit sufficient funds to cover this closing fee. You are responsible for this bank fee; therefore, you must not allow client funds to cover it.

Step 4. Prepare and send any final client bills.

Step 5. Disburse any funds belonging to your law firm, such as earned fees and reimbursement for any client costs advanced.

Step 6. Disburse funds belonging to clients by sending a check from the trust account to the client with the final bill, or, if the client directs this, send the balance to the client's new law firm with a cover letter, with a copy to your client.

Step 7. If you have been unable to reach your client to return any funds owed to your client, you need to consult with your state bar association or provincial law society in order to comply with any rules regarding unclaimed property. Your state or province will likely have an unclaimed property statute, which will need to be followed.

a. If you have clients and unclaimed funds in more than one jurisdiction, check with each appropriate jurisdiction to follow its rules. One state may require filing a report with the Division of State Land, while another state may require filing a report with the State Treasurer's Office. One state requires turning the money over to your state's Law Foundation running your state's IOLTA program, while another state requires turning the money over to the State Treasurer's Office or Division of State Land. In Canada, you would turn over any unclaimed trust funds to your Provincial Law Society. You need to check what applies in your situation.

b. In no event is it proper for you to convert your client's property to your own.
c. Also note if you will need to file any subsequent reports concerning this unclaimed property so you can comply.
d. Confirm what to do if your client reappears and wants the money so that your client is assisted in getting his or her money refunded. In Canada, you would have your client contact the local law society.

Step 8. Do not close your trust account at the bank until all outstanding checks have cleared.

Step 9. Be sure to shred any unused checks and deposit slips to prevent fraud and to protect you from accidentally using any checks and deposit slips from this closed account.

Step 10. Check with your appropriate jurisdiction for the rules that apply regarding keeping records of your trust account. Determine what you are required to keep regarding your account, such as any check register or equivalent report detailing transactions, bank statements (whether they are allowed to be kept in electronic form or required to be kept in paper), client ledgers, or equivalent reports detailing transactions for each individual client. Determine how long to preserve client trust account records after termination of representation. In Canada, the minimum record retention time is ten years; this may be extended when minors are involved or there are other special considerations. Check with your local law society.

a. If you do not preserve these records for the required time, you will be violating your ethics rules and could incur disciplinary action.
b. If you are officially resigning from being a lawyer in your jurisdiction, carefully determine what is required as part of this resignation process. Part of the process of resignation may require that you affirm to comply with all your ethics rules. So arguably, the court with jurisdiction over you could prosecute you for not obeying a court order.

Guiding Rules and Concepts

Client Money Belongs in the Trust Account

Until you have earned your fees, the money in your trust account held on behalf of a particular client belongs to that client. If you receive settlement proceeds that belong partly to you and partly to your client, or partly to someone else and partly to your client, likely you will receive one check covering both shares. Deposit this check into the trust account and wait until the funds have been collected and are actually available in the trust account before issuing checks.

If your jurisdiction allows "earned upon receipt" funds, these do not go into your trust account. The operative word is *earned*. Because it is earned, it belongs to you and therefore belongs in your law firm's operating account.

> **Practice Tip:** *If your client pays costs and fees up front, before costs are incurred and fees are earned, the money still belongs to your client, and it should be deposited into a client trust account.*

Never Commingle Funds

You must not commingle your money with your client's money. You will need to open a minimum of two bank accounts: a general operating account in which you hold money belonging to your law firm and a client trust account in which you hold money belonging to your client. Even if you are a solo, you still need these two accounts.

In Canada, there is no requirement to open a trust account; in some cases you can use the trust account of a colleague to hold trust funds on an "as needed" basis.

You will also need to have a personal checking account with which to pay for your personal expenses that are not related to the law firm, such as your mortgage, groceries, and medical expenses. This means you will write a check from the client trust account to pay the law firm for earned fees. You will then write a check from the law firm general operating account to yourself to pay your salary. Ultimately, you will write a check from your personal checking account to pay your monthly car payment.

You never should write a trust account check to pay for your bar dues or pay for your car repair, even if you are owed money from the account. Keep things properly segregated by establishing a general operating account for your law practice, a client trust account for holding client funds, and a personal bank account for paying non–law firm expenses.

You cannot have money in your trust account that belongs to you unless it is solely for covering the bank service fees, and it should not be more at any one time than is reasonably necessary for that purpose. Some jurisdictions will also allow you to keep your money in the client trust account for maintaining the bank's minimum balance requirements to avoid fees or service charges. Check what the rules are in your jurisdiction.

Model Rule 1.15(b) provides that it is permissible to commingle your funds with clients when necessary for the sole purpose of paying the bank service charges but only in the amount for that purpose. If you do so, you need to keep accurate records regarding what part of the funds in your trust account belongs to you. Keep bank records to substantiate these service charges. Check with your own jurisdiction's rules to be clear on what is allowed. For example, British Columbia allows lawyers to keep up to $300 of their own funds in their trust account to help offset bank service charges and banking errors.

> **Practice Tip:** *Fees are yours upon being earned. Do not leave your money in your client trust account; it is not a savings account. Withdraw earned funds within a reasonable time to avoid the impermissible commingling of your funds with your clients' funds. Do not deposit your money into your trust account except in an amount necessary to cover bank fees.*

Treat Each Client as a Separate Trust Account

As far as your bank is concerned, you have one trust account, usually an IOLTA account, holding a given sum at any given time. But it's your responsibility to keep up with each client and third party whose money you hold, and to know exactly how much you are holding for each of them. These client trust accounts are subaccounts of the overall trust account that the bank holds on deposit under one account number.

Treat each client as a separate account. If you think of it this way, you will be more inclined to pay the proper attention to your client trust account.

If Client Smith doesn't have enough money in your trust account, you wouldn't dream of "borrowing" money from Client Brown's trust account funds to pay for Client Smith's legal fees. But that is what you will do if the funds in Client Smith's subaccount have not been collected before you begin writing checks. You are headed for trouble if you do!

You may not realize you are using other clients' money because your focus is on the balance of the overall client trust account. An overdraft in your client trust account can usually be traced back to improper monitoring of funds in each client subaccount.

Practice Tip: *Be sure to properly set up subaccounts in your trust account, one for each client, and review the subaccount before withdrawing any money on behalf of that client.*

Track Individual Client Subaccounts Carefully

You need to keep track of the overall trust account funds and the funds of each client subaccount. If you take good care in tracking your individual client trust subaccounts, you will have a much easier time keeping track of the overall trust account in the bank.

In earlier times, each client's trust account money was tracked on a buff-colored client ledger card that showed the opening deposit of the client's money received in trust, any costs advanced by the law firm, and any legal fees for services charged. The ledger card would also show when money was disbursed from the trust account to first pay for costs advanced and then for legal fees charged. These are reflected as advanced costs received and fees received.

Ideally the balance in the client trust account is enough to reduce the costs advanced balance amount to zero and to reduce the fees accounts receivable balance to zero monthly.

If your fee agreement provides for it, you may want to request a replenishing deposit from your client to bring the trust account balance up to a required level; otherwise, you will no longer have client funds held in trust with which to pay ongoing costs and fees during the duration of the client matter. Consider the use of an evergreen retainer provision that requires the client to replenish the retainer to the stated amount each month after it is depleted to pay costs and fees.

At any given time, the client ledger must show how much is held in the client trust account for that client and itemize receipt of funds on behalf of the client along with fees and costs incurred and paid on behalf of the client. Note if you maintain electronic records of each client sub account in your accounting program for tracking all transactions in your client's trust account, be diligent about recording all transactions contemporaneously. You always want to know to the penny how much money is held for each client.

Today many lawyers use accounting software programs such as QuickBooks to track their trust account and each of their individual clients' subaccounts. Accounting software programs, or trust accounting features of all-in-one legal-specific practice management programs, provide reporting capabilities so that a trust account report can be set up to report separately for each of the client subaccounts, giving the complete accounting details that have always been necessary.

> **Practice Tip:** *Get in the good habit of doing your banking and billing at a regular time of month, and take money from your client trust account after it is earned and the client is notified on the monthly statement issued to your client in accordance with your fee agreement.*

Whose Money Is It?

The key concept is ownership of the funds. Until the lawyer has earned the money, it belongs to the client, and client money belongs in the trust account.

Check with your jurisdiction for the specific requirements regarding transferring funds from your trust account to your general account or using trust funds to pay disbursements to cover the client's expenses.

In Canada, it is a requirement to render an invoice to the client prior to transferring any funds from the trust account to the general account, even if it is only to pay disbursements. In other jurisdictions, it is permissible to notify the client of your procedures for handling trust account funds in the signed engagement letter; then the lawyer can withdraw trust funds as they are earned or costs are incurred. If the client disputes fees or costs, then the lawyer would replace the amount disputed back into the trust account.

If the lawyer advances costs, such as by paying filing fees at the time the court documents are filed, then at the next billing period the lawyer can and should withdraw that amount from the trust account to reimburse the law firm, unless in Canada, where the client must receive the invoice before removing funds.

Note that if court filing fees must be paid electronically at the time of e-filing, you will want to have a law firm credit card to use for paying court filing fees through the secure online portal. If you use a debit card, see that it is connected to your general operating account, never to your client trust account—this would be a dangerous idea, opening yourself to unauthorized use of client funds. In Canada, it is a breach of the trust accounting rules to withdraw funds from a trust account via an ATM.

Is it wrong to write a check from the client trust account directly to court? No, as long as the court expense has been incurred. Essentially, you are paying the obligations of the client with the client's money. Courts are less likely to accept any checks, requiring that if filing into a case electronically, the accompanying filing fees must be paid electronically as well, which means lawyers are using a credit card for the law firm for filing fees in eCourt.

Keep accurate records of what you pay, when you pay, and on whose behalf you pay. To keep records more easily, write checks from the client trust account at month-end when you send your billing statement to show the client what legal services you performed, what legal costs have been incurred, the amount withdrawn from the client's trust account, and the balance remaining after legal fees and legal costs have been paid.

> **Practice Tip:** *Never use an ATM card linked to the trust account. Instead, advance costs from your general account and then reimburse the firm from the trust account. An ATM card makes it too easy to withdraw money without creating the detailed record that is generated when writing a check, and it opens the door for embezzlement. In Canada, it is a breach of the trust accounting rules to withdraw trust funds via an ATM.*

Wait an Adequate Time Before Disbursing Trust Funds

Confused by banking terminology? Instead of asking whether funds are "cleared" or funds are "available," ask if the funds have been "collected and are available to be withdrawn" from your account. This will let you know that the actual amount of the deposit is really in your account and can be withdrawn without impacting any other money that is in there.

Why is this important? Usually banks will provide a certain amount of money for withdrawal based on what is in the account already. If you withdraw money deposited before it is actually in the account, you are withdrawing money belonging to other clients.

Some jurisdictions will allow you to go ahead and disburse against uncollected funds in your trust account, as long as you are willing and able to reimburse the trust account from your own funds if a deposit you have made is dishonored. But do you really ever want to use your own money to cover for a client who has given you a bad check? Most jurisdictions will require that your bank report to the bar if a check drawn on a client trust account bounces or if an overdraft has been created. Many of these jurisdictions require the lawyer to self-report to the bar upon notification by the bank that a check has bounced or an overdraft has been created. Do you have to self-report if a deposit made to your trust account is dishonored, or rejected by the issuing bank? You will need to check, but generally the self-reporting requirement is for checks that you yourself bounce, since a bouncing check from a client is not in your control.

Some jurisdictions, such as Canada, make it a requirement you must immediately deposit back to trust any shortfalls in your trust account. Furthermore, shortages in your trust account must be reported to your regulator forthwith if they are over a certain threshold, such as the $2,500 current threshold in British Columbia.

To be prudent, allow sufficient time for funds deposited to become available. How long should you wait? Check with your jurisdiction for guidelines; if there are none, contact your local financial institution for advice. For example, in Oregon we advise lawyers to adopt the 3-5-10 day rule. Before using deposited funds, wait three banking days after depositing a check drawn on a bank located in the same city where your trust account is held, five banking days on a bank located in the same state, and ten banking days on a bank located out of state. A banking day is a day on which a bank is open to the public for carrying on the business of its banking functions, typically Monday through Friday, except for legally defined holidays. Some lawyers simplify this to waiting ten banking days after depositing any check before using the funds. Because of the current ability of fraudsters to counterfeit even cashier's checks with great accuracy, you may wish to contact the bank on which a check is drawn to determine that it is genuine before depositing it.

Practice Tip: *Establish a prudent policy of allowing adequate time for your deposit to become available, such as the 3-5-10 day rule, and stick to your policy.*

The Buck Stops with You

Although it is not in your control whether a client or other third party issues a good check to be deposited into your trust account, it is in your control to safeguard money belonging to someone else. Realize that if a deposited check bounces and you have drawn on its funds, you have wrongfully used money belonging to your other clients.

Check if your jurisdiction requires you to report to the bar if you have been notified that a deposit item has been returned. Your local jurisdiction may only get a report from the bank if a check drawn on the trust account bounces or is paid and creates an overdraft. Your jurisdiction may not allow overdraft protection for your trust account, likely because then the bar would not be notified that an overdraft situation had existed. Whatever the reason, if your jurisdiction does not allow it, don't do it.

When it comes to your trust account, think strict liability: the buck stops with you. There are no excuses.

What might happen to you? After your bank notifies you and your bar's regulatory services, you might be obligated to self-report to the bar. If so, comply promptly. Otherwise, you may be suspected of not being aware of what is going on with your trust account and disciplined. Will bar regulatory authority then warn you to be more careful, put you into a discipline diversion program, put you on probation, issue a public reprimand, or suspend you from practicing law? It all depends on all the facts in your situation. But one thing is for sure: don't find out. Properly manage your client trust account and avoid embarrassing problems.

Practice Tip: *Beware! Any time you pay out deposited funds before they are collected and in your account, you are spending other clients' money.*

Don't Spend What You Don't Have

Suppose you are just about to settle your case. You have the opposing counsel's word that a good settlement offer is imminent, and the client had talked about how much he wanted when he first came into your office.

You don't have authorization—yet—to settle but are totally confident that once you present the settlement offer to your client, your client will accept. Just in time. Payroll is due and everyone, especially you, needs the money.

Going back to the office, you write a check from the trust account to cover the amount of this month's payroll. You call your client and leave a message about the great news. The nice story doesn't end as you planned. Either the client now has a different settlement offer in mind or the opposing counsel has exaggerated the amount. Either way, you have jumped the gun and pulled out money belonging to your clients to cover your payroll expense.

Until the settlement is offered and accepted and deposited into your trust account and the settlement funds are collected and in your account, you cannot spend the money. Ethically you are in a bad position and should consult ethics counsel for help with what to do when you have spent what you don't have.

It Looks like a Check, but It's a Bank Draft

A bank draft is a type of check where the payment is guaranteed to be available by the issuing bank. Once the bank has confirmed that sufficient funds are available, the issuing bank sets aside the funds from the person's account to be paid over when the bank draft is presented by the receiving bank. The problem may arise when the issuing bank reviews the way the draft was endorsed, refuses to pay based on an improper endorsement, and sends it back as a dishonored draft. If the dishonored draft comes back to your trust account, then you don't have the money until the endorsement is corrected and the draft is re-presented to the issuing bank.

> **Practice Tip:** *Insurance companies frequently use drafts instead of checks. Be careful when handling this type of payment. Ask your bank to notify you when the funds have been collected and properly credited to your account.*

Account for Every Penny

As long as the funds remain in your possession, you must account for every penny. You need to be accurate and scrupulously honest. You must not invent charges to make your trust account balance.

Handle your client's funds with extreme care. You may not intentionally mishandle your client's funds, but you can have a terrible mistake happen if you aren't careful enough.

To prevent mishandling your trust account, account for every penny. Most mishandling events are caused by failing to keep proper records. You may subject your client to economic hardship and yourself to sanctions for ethics violations, and you will seriously undermine the public's confidence in the legal profession.

> **Practice Tip:** *Get into the habit of recording all deposits and withdrawals at the time you write the deposit slip or check and notate the client ledger card or its electronic equivalent accordingly.*

Maintain a Clear Audit Trail

Keep complete records of your trust account, including checkbooks, check stubs, deposit slips, statements from the bank, client billing statements, vouchers, receipts, or statements that substantiate what costs were paid. In this day of electronic banking, most banks will not return cancelled checks and may charge extra to provide paper statements. Check with your jurisdiction to determine whether you are allowed to rely on electronic statements instead of paper ones.

If your bank does not return cancelled checks or provide monthly bank statements by mail, be sure to access your account online and print your monthly statement or save it in a PDF format. If you have PDF creation software like Adobe Acrobat, select Adobe PDF as the printer and then print. You will have created a PDF of this document without printing it and then scanning it, saving paper, time, and energy.

Be able to get an electronic copy of your checks and deposit items. These are important to capture. Although your bank will allow you to retrieve your electronic banking records, usually it will only allow you to go back 24 months, which may not be a sufficient time for you to maintain these records in your jurisdiction. The ABA Model Rules require you to maintain these records for a minimum of five years, while in Canada you must maintain them for a minimum of ten years.

If your bank allows you to make telephone, electronic, or wire transfers to and from the trust account, these types of transactions generally do not generate a clear audit trail to substantiate whose money was transferred and for what purpose. Keep contemporaneous records to document any transfers. In Canada, telephone transfers and ATM transfers from the trust account to the general account are not allowed. Even if telephone transfers or ATM transfers from the trust account to the general account are allowed in your jurisdiction, you should seriously consider refraining from doing so.

Many lawyers have made trust accounting errors after doing a telephone transfer from the trust account to the general operating account because they did not keep contemporaneous record to document this action; then they forgot that they did a telephone transfer and later took the same amount in the month by writing a check from their trust account and depositing it into their general operating account. Be very careful to always document transactions concerning your trust account so you do not inadvertently withdraw the same amount twice. To your horror, you may find that an overdraft has resulted.

This unfortunate situation and other similar mishaps are avoidable if you immediately document all transactions. Don't be in too big of a hurry and think you can do this later, as it is easy to get caught up in another distraction. Consider creating a form to track any telephone or wire transfers, and then be sure to use it. Get into the good habit of keeping contemporaneous electronic records of all your banking transactions. Do you have a special time of day for handling financial matters? Taking care of everything at one time can be a helpful practice for staying current and accurate with all your banking accounts.

Remember that an ABA Model Rule 1.15 comment [1] states, "A lawyer should maintain on a current basis books and records in accordance with generally accepted accounting practice and comply with any recordkeeping rules established by law or court order. See e.g., ABA Model Rules for Client Trust Account Records."

> **Practice Tip:** *Be able to substantiate everything having to do with your client trust account.*

Never Have a Negative Balance

Your client's funds held in your trust account will eventually be reduced to zero, but never to a negative balance. At some point, you will close out your client trust account, and there must be a zero balance because there is no longer any client funds, or there will be the nominal amount of money that you were allowed to hold in the trust account to pay bank charges. If you have a negative balance at the time the account is being closed, or at any time, you have done something seriously wrong or there has been a theft.

> **Practice Tip:** *Be scrupulous in handling your trust account, and you should never find a negative balance either for your trust account or for any individual client's subaccount.*

The Duty to Account to Your Client

You are a fiduciary when it comes to your client's money. You have a duty to account to your client about how much money you received on behalf of your client, when you received it, and from whom.

When you pay a cost on behalf of your client, whether by paying with a trust account check or by advancing the cost with funds from your general operating account, make a copy of the billing from the vendor and any receipt given and include these copies with your monthly statement.

Your client expects a monthly statement from you along with all the other monthly statements your client receives. At minimum, send a statement every month there is a transaction in the trust account.

Your monthly statement should show the balance forward in the client's trust subaccount, costs paid either directly from the trust account or, if advanced by your law firm, the amount being reimbursed to your law firm, an itemization of your time charges with enough detail so that the client understands what you have done on the client's behalf, any additional deposits from the client to increase the client trust account balance or settlement proceeds received, and the ending balance.

The Duty to Safeguard Your Client's Property

You are a fiduciary, entrusted with safeguarding your client's money by your client. Keeping it safe requires more than just depositing it into your client trust account. It requires you to put safety measures in place to guard against fraud or embezzlement, especially if you delegate certain bookkeeping duties.

Here are some trust account safeguards to consider adopting:

1. Never, ever use a signature stamp.
2. Control access to checkbooks and unused check supply.
3. Review all client billings and receipts of payment.
4. Never sign a check without reviewing adequate supporting documentation.
5. Divide up duties. One staff opens mail with you in the morning. Together, you stamp all checks received with your account's endorsement stamp: "pay to the order of [stamp]." The person who pays the bills should not be the same person who reconciles the bank accounts.
6. Consider having the bank statement mailed to your house, or, if you receive an electronic statement, safeguard your password to access your account.
7. Even if you use a bookkeeper, review your trust account records carefully every month.
8. Handle cash received cautiously. Have at least one other person witness all cash payments received, and have both the witness and client sign and date the receipt. Give a copy to your client and keep the other copy in your account records.
    a. NOTE: There are strict laws concerning the reproduction of United States paper currency as a deterrent to counterfeiting. Do not make a photocopy of cash payments without checking out what is allowed in your jurisdiction.
9. Consider requiring two signatures on large checks, such as on amounts over $10,000 or even $5,000. I would recommend requiring two signatures on any check issued in $5,000. The

goal isn't to impede the orderly handling of checks but to put the brakes on checks being issued without considered oversight. Your internal policy on checks should be that no check is signed unless it is presented with the underlying documentation of the incurred expense. Though you can't rely on your bank to enforce the two-signature rule, it is an effective internal control because it encourages people to pay closer attention to the check-writing process. For checks drawn on the trust account, consider requiring that a printout of the client's ledger card or its electronic equivalent be presented along with the evidence of the underlying expense. This may help prevent you from drawing down on a client's subaccount when there are not adequate funds to cover the expense, resulting in using another client's money to cover the expense.

10. If you have different trust accounts for clients in different states, or more than one pooled trust account (such as one for real estate and another for general matters or litigation), select different-colored checks and prominently write the state or account name on the checkbook cover.
11. If you do online banking, be sure that your computer is up-to-date with the latest anti-malware, anti-virus protection, and run a scan before accessing your bank account online.
12. Be careful when receiving an unusually large cashier's check from a new client, especially if it is just before a bank holiday, because this is the most popular time for fraudsters to scam you with a counterfeit cashier's check. Typically, the fraudster overpays by a significant amount and then demands a refund of the overage. By the time your bank notifies you that the cashier's check is counterfeit, the fraudster is long gone and your trust account is short a few thousand dollars, or worse.

The Duty to Return Your Client's Property

It is your client's money. If you don't complete the work for which you have been paid in advance, then you must return the unearned money. Most states consider that the client file belongs to the client unless you have already provided the client with a complete client file, and then the file at your law office is your law office's file.

Usually, the law firm is busy working on the client's behalf and the client is getting copies of letters sent out by the law firm. Period. The client frequently isn't getting copies of letters received by the law firm. And e-mail, which is just correspondence of a different form, is not being copied for the client.

So consider what may happen if the relationship sours between you and your client. Whether justified or not, your client fires you and wants to go to another lawyer and demands a copy of his client file. Angry, you think, "Over my dead body am I giving you this client file." You do nothing. Or you don't know how to respond or are embarrassed by the disorganization of that client file. You do nothing. Your client is anxious and angry and files a bar complaint. You now need to respond to the bar, and this takes two drafts before your reply is suitable for being read by your bar's client assistance officer or disciplinary counsel. You confide this to your former law school classmate, who encourages you to consult local ethics counsel, and this takes time. Then there is all the time you spend being indignant that your client has had the audacity to file a bar complaint because you didn't send him his client file, which doesn't even have a lot in it that would be of use to another attorney. You are losing money by delaying.

Check with your jurisdiction on what constitutes the client file. Many states have adopted the entire file theory that everything in the file belongs to the client.

Even if your jurisdiction has not adopted the entire file theory, your most affordable course of action is to copy the entire client file and send it to your client or, at your client's direction, to your client's new lawyer. Your time and professional reputation are too valuable to waste in creating client misunderstandings and ill will. Remove any sample work product belonging to another client you held in the file. Also remove any internal memorandum commenting on the client. Remove any correspondence between you and your malpractice carrier regarding the case. Likewise, establish a separate bar complaint folder pertaining to this client.

All that should be in the file is the work you have done on your client's behalf for which your client has paid. If your client owes you money, try to get your client to your bar's fee arbitration program, if you have one.

Do not hold your client's file hostage for unpaid fees. You cannot do something that causes harm to your client or fail to do something that causes harm to your client. Thou shalt not harm your client. Run around the block and let this go; you have work to do.

Practice Tip: *In Canada, check with your regulator, or in the United States with your regulatory agency, who may be able to provide assistance on what to return to the client and what to retain.*

Conclusion

Protecting client and third-party property obtained in connection with a representation requires that you promptly deposit funds into your trust account and otherwise keep accurate records of property received and returned. Being diligent about maintaining proper records is how you fulfill your obligation to protect your client's property.

If asked, can you immediately tell your client how much money is held in your trust account on his or her behalf? You should keep such good records that you can determine exactly how much money you hold for each client within minutes.

If your trust account records are in a jumble, you are more apt to get into trouble. Hopefully, after reading this book you now know how to get a handle on your trust account. Don't ignore any problems you are encountering with managing your trust account. They usually compound and get harder to resolve the longer you let them remain outstanding.

If you need help beyond the information in this book, contact your bar's ethics counsel or a practice management advisor who will be available to help you. The next section gives resources for getting further help.

Resources

- **ABA Directory of IOLTA Programs** — www.americanbar.org/groups/interest_lawyers_trust_accounts/resources/directory_of_iolta_programs.html
- **ABA Legal Technology Resource Center** — www.americanbar.org/groups/departments_offices/legal_technology_resources.html
- **ABA Model Rules** — www.americanbar.org/groups/professional_responsibility/publications/model_rules_of_professional_conduct/model_rules_of_professional_conduct_table_of_contents.html
- **ABA Model Rules for Client Trust Account Records** — www.americanbar.org/content/dam/aba/migrated/cpr/clientpro/adopted_8_10_10.authcheckdam.pdf
- **ABA Law Practice Division: Practice Management Advisors/State and Local Bar Outreach Committee — PMAs of North America** — https://apps.americanbar.org/dch/committee.cfm?com=EP024000
- **Federation Model Code of Professional Conduct — Federation of Law Societies of Canada** — http://flsc.ca/wp-content/uploads/2014/12/Model-Code-as-amended-march-2016-FINAL.pdf
- **Interactive Model Code of Professional Conduct with Equivalent Provincial/Territorial Provisions** — http://flsc.ca/interactivecode/

APPENDIX A

ABA Model Rules for Professional Conduct

February 2013

Rule 1.15: Safekeeping Property with Comments

http://www.americanbar.org/groups/professional_responsibility/publications/model_rules_of_professional_conduct/rule_1_15_safekeeping_property.html

MODEL RULES FOR PROFESSIONAL CONDUCT RULE 1.15: SAFEKEEPING PROPERTY

Client-Lawyer Relationship

RULE 1.15 SAFEKEEPING PROPERTY

(a) A lawyer shall hold property of clients or third persons that is in a lawyer's possession in connection with a representation separate from the lawyer's own property. Funds shall be kept in a separate account maintained in the state where the lawyer's office is situated, or elsewhere with the consent of the client or third person. Other property shall be identified as such and appropriately safeguarded. Complete records of such account funds and other property shall be kept by the lawyer and shall be preserved for a period of [five years] after termination of the representation.

(b) A lawyer may deposit the lawyer's own funds in a client trust account for the sole purpose of paying bank service charges on that account, but only in an amount necessary for that purpose.

(c) A lawyer shall deposit into a client trust account legal fees and expenses that have been paid in advance, to be withdrawn by the lawyer only as fees are earned or expenses incurred.

(d) Upon receiving funds or other property in which a client or third person has an interest, a lawyer shall promptly notify the client or third person. Except as stated in this rule or otherwise permitted by law or by agreement with the client, a lawyer shall promptly deliver to the client or third person any funds or other property that the client or third person is entitled to receive and, upon request by the client or third person, shall promptly render a full accounting regarding such property.

(e) When in the course of representation a lawyer is in possession of property in which two or more persons (one of whom may be the lawyer) claim interests, the property shall be kept separate by the lawyer until the dispute is resolved. The lawyer shall promptly distribute all portions of the property as to which the interests are not in dispute.

COMMENT

Rule 1.15 Safekeeping Property—Comment

[1] A lawyer should hold property of others with the care required of a professional fiduciary. Securities should be kept in a safe deposit box, except when some other form of safekeeping is warranted by special circumstances. All property that is the property of clients or third persons, including prospective clients, must be kept separate from the lawyer's

business and personal property and, if monies, in one or more trust accounts. Separate trust accounts may be warranted when administering estate monies or acting in similar fiduciary capacities. A lawyer should maintain on a current basis books and records in accordance with generally accepted accounting practice and comply with any recordkeeping rules established by law or court order. See, e.g., Model Rules for Client Trust Account Records.

[2] While normally it is impermissible to commingle the lawyer's own funds with client funds, paragraph (b) provides that it is permissible when necessary to pay bank service charges on that account. Accurate records must be kept regarding which part of the funds are the lawyer's.

[3] Lawyers often receive funds from which the lawyer's fee will be paid. The lawyer is not required to remit to the client funds that the lawyer reasonably believes represent fees owed. However, a lawyer may not hold funds to coerce a client into accepting the lawyer's contention. The disputed portion of the funds must be kept in a trust account and the lawyer should suggest means for prompt resolution of the dispute, such as arbitration. The undisputed portion of the funds shall be promptly distributed.

[4] Paragraph (e) also recognizes that third parties may have lawful claims against specific funds or other property in a lawyer's custody, such as a client's creditor who has a lien on funds recovered in a personal injury action. A lawyer may have a duty under applicable law to protect such third-party claims against wrongful interference by the client. In such cases, when the third-party claim is not frivolous under applicable law, the lawyer must refuse to surrender the property to the client until the claims are resolved. A lawyer should not unilaterally assume to arbitrate a dispute between the client and the third party, but, when there are substantial grounds for dispute as to the person entitled to the funds, the lawyer may file an action to have a court resolve the dispute.

[5] The obligations of a lawyer under this Rule are independent of those arising from activity other than rendering legal services. For example, a lawyer who serves only as an escrow agent is governed by the applicable law relating to fiduciaries even though the lawyer does not render legal services in the transaction and is not governed by this Rule.

[6] A lawyers' fund for client protection provides a means through the collective efforts of the bar to reimburse persons who have lost money or property as a result of dishonest conduct of a lawyer. Where such a fund has been established, a lawyer must participate where it is mandatory, and, even when it is voluntary, the lawyer should participate.

APPENDIX B

Federation Model Code of Professional Conduct

As Amended March 10, 2016

http://flsc.ca/wp-content/uploads/2014/12/Model-Code-as-amended-march-2016-FINAL.pdf [see pages 62–63]

Rule 3.5: Preservation of Clients' Property with Commentary

Preservation of Clients' Property

3.5-1 In this rule, "**property**" includes a client's money, securities as defined in [provincial legislation], original documents such as wills, title deeds, minute books, licences, certificates and the like, and all other papers such as client's correspondence, files, reports, invoices and other such documents, as well as personal property including precious and semi-precious metals, jewellery and the like.

3.5-2 A lawyer must:

(a) care for a client's property as a careful and prudent owner would when dealing with like property; and

(b) observe all relevant rules and law about the preservation of a client's property entrusted to a lawyer.

COMMENTARY

[1] The duties concerning safekeeping, preserving, and accounting for clients' monies and other property are set out in the [rules/regulations/by-laws of the relevant Law Society].

[2] These duties are closely related to those regarding confidential information. A lawyer is responsible for maintaining the safety and confidentiality of the files of the client in the possession of the lawyer and should take all reasonable steps to ensure the privacy and safekeeping of a client's confidential information. A lawyer should keep the client's papers and other property out of sight as well as out of reach of those not entitled to see them.

[3] Subject to any rights of lien, the lawyer should promptly return a client's property to the client on request or at the conclusion of the lawyer's retainer.

[4] If the lawyer withdraws from representing a client, the lawyer is required to comply with Rule 3.7-1 (Withdrawal from Representation).

Notification of Receipt of Property

3.5-3 A lawyer must promptly notify a client of the receipt of any money or other property of the client, unless satisfied that the client is aware that they have come into the lawyer's custody.

Identifying Clients' Property

3.5-4 A lawyer must clearly label and identify clients' property and place it in safekeeping distinguishable from the lawyer's own property.

3.5-5 A lawyer must maintain such records as necessary to identify clients' property that is in the lawyer's custody.

Accounting and Delivery

3.5-6 A lawyer must account promptly for clients' property that is in the lawyer's custody and deliver it to the order of the client on request or, if appropriate, at the conclusion of the retainer.

3.5-7 If a lawyer is unsure of the proper person to receive a client's property, the lawyer must apply to a tribunal of competent jurisdiction for direction.

COMMENTARY

[1] A lawyer should be alert to the duty to claim on behalf of a client any privilege in respect of property seized or attempted to be seized by an external authority or in respect of third party claims made against the property. In this regard, the lawyer should be familiar with the nature of the client's common law privilege and with such relevant constitutional and statutory provisions as those found in the Income Tax Act (Canada), the Charter and the Criminal Code.

ABA Model Rules for Client Trust Account Records

Rule 1: Recordkeeping Generally with Comments
www.americanbar.org/content/dam/aba/migrated/cpr/clientpro/adopted_8_10_10.authcheckdam.pdf

MODEL RULES FOR CLIENT TRUST ACCOUNT RECORDS

Adopted by the American Bar Association House of Delegates on August 9, 2010

Rule 1: Recordkeeping Generally

A lawyer who practices in this jurisdiction shall maintain current financial records as provided in these Rules and required by [Rule 1.15 of the Model Rules of Professional Conduct], and shall retain the following records for a period of [five years] after termination of the representation:

(a) receipt and disbursement journals containing a record of deposits to and withdrawals from client trust accounts, specifically identifying the date, source, and description of each item deposited, as well as the date, payee and purpose of each disbursement;

(b) ledger records for all client trust accounts showing, for each separate trust client or beneficiary, the source of all funds deposited, the names of all persons for whom the funds are or were held, the amount of such funds, the descriptions and amounts of charges or withdrawals, and the names of all persons or entities to whom such funds were disbursed;

(c) copies of retainer and compensation agreements with clients [as required by Rule 1.5 of the Model Rules of Professional Conduct];

(d) copies of accountings to clients or third persons showing the disbursement of funds to them or on their behalf;

(e) copies of bills for legal fees and expenses rendered to clients;

(f) copies of records showing disbursements on behalf of clients;

(g) the physical or electronic equivalents of all checkbook registers, bank statements, records of deposit, pre-numbered canceled checks, and substitute checks provided by a financial institution;

(h) records of all electronic transfers from client trust accounts, including the name of the person authorizing transfer, the date of transfer, the name of the recipient and confirmation from the financial institution of the trust account number from which money was withdrawn and the date and the time the transfer was completed;

(i) copies of [monthly] trial balances and [quarterly] reconciliations of the client trust accounts maintained by the lawyer; and

(j) copies of those portions of client files that are reasonably related to client trust account transactions.

COMMENT:

[1] Rule 1 enumerates the basic financial records that a lawyer must maintain with regard to all trust accounts of a law firm. These include

the standard books of account, and the supporting records that are necessary to safeguard and account for the receipt and disbursement of client or third person funds as required by Rule 1.15 of the Model Rules of Professional Conduct or its equivalent. Consistent with Rule 1.15, this Rule proposes that lawyers maintain client trust account records for a period of five years after termination of each particular legal engagement or representation. Although these Model Rules address the accepted use of a client trust account by a lawyer when holding client or third person funds, some jurisdictions may permit a lawyer to deposit certain advance fees for legal services into the lawyer's business or operating account. In those situations, the lawyer should still be guided by the standards contained in these Model Rules.

[2] Rule 1(g) requires that the physical or electronic equivalents of all checkbook registers, bank statements, records of deposit, pre-numbered canceled checks, and substitute checks be maintained for a period of five years after termination of each legal engagement or representation. The "Check Clearing for the 21st Century Act" or "Check 21 Act", codified at 12 U.S.C.§5001 et. seq., recognizes "substitute checks" as the legal equivalent of an original check. A "substitute check" is defined at 12 U.S.C. §5002(16) as "paper reproduction of the original check that contains an image of the front and back of the original check; bears a magnetic ink character recognition ("MICR") line containing all the information appearing on the MICR line of the original check; conforms with generally applicable industry standards for substitute checks; and is suitable for automated processing in the same manner as the original check. Banks, as defined in 12 U.S.C. §5002(2), are not required to return to customers the original canceled checks. Most banks now provide electronic images of checks to customers who have access to their accounts on internet-based websites. It is the lawyer's responsibility to download electronic images. Electronic images shall be maintained for the requisite number of years and shall be readily available for printing

upon request or shall be printed and maintained for the requisite number of years.

[3] The ACH (Automated Clearing House) Network is an electronic funds transfer or payment system that primarily provides for the interbank clearing of electronic payments between originating and receiving participating financial institutions. ACH transactions are payment instructions to either debit or credit a deposit account. ACH payments are used in a variety of payment environments including bill payments, business-to-business payments, and government payments (e.g. tax refunds.) In addition to the primary use of ACH transactions, retailers and third parties use the ACH system for other types of transactions including electronic check conversion (ECC). ECC is the process of transmitting MICR information from the bottom of a check, converting check payments to ACH transactions depending upon the authorization given by the account holder at the point-of-purchase. In this type of transaction, the lawyer should be careful to comply with the requirements of Rule 1(h).

[4] There are five types of check conversions where a lawyer should be careful to comply with the requirements of Rule 1(h). First, in a "point-of-purchase conversion," a paper check is converted into a debit at the point of purchase and the paper check is returned to the issuer. Second, in a "back-office conversion," a paper check is presented at the point of purchase and is later converted into a debit and the paper check is destroyed. Third, in an "account-receivable conversion," a paper check is converted into a debit and the paper check is destroyed. Fourth, in a "telephone-initiated debit" or "check-by-phone" conversion, bank account information is provided via the telephone and the information is converted to a debit. Fifth, in a "web-initiated debit," an electronic payment is initiated through a secure web environment. Rule 1(h) applies to each of the type of electronic funds transfers described.

All electronic funds transfers shall be recorded and a lawyer should not re-use a check number which has been previously used in an electronic transfer transaction.

[5] The potential of these records to serve as safeguards is realized only if the procedures set forth in Rule 1(i) are regularly performed. The trial balance is the sum of balances of each client's ledger card (or the electronic equivalent). Its value lies in comparing it on a monthly basis to a control balance. The control balance starts with the previous month's balance, then adds receipts from the Trust Receipts Journal and subtracts disbursements from the Trust Disbursements Journal. Once the total matches the trial balance, the reconciliation readily follows by adding amounts of any outstanding checks and subtracting any deposits not credited by the bank at month's end. This balance should agree with the bank statement. Quarterly reconciliation is recommended only as a minimum requirement; monthly reconciliation is the preferred practice given the difficulty of identifying an error (whether by the lawyer or the bank) among three months' transactions.

[6] In some situations, documentation in addition to that listed in paragraphs (a) through (i) of Rule 1 is necessary for a complete understanding of a trust account transaction. The type of document that a lawyer must retain under paragraph (j) because it is "reasonably related" to a client trust transaction will vary depending on the nature of the transaction and the significance of the document in shedding light on the transaction. Examples of documents that typically must be retained under this paragraph include correspondence between the client and lawyer relating to a disagreement over fees or costs or the distribution of proceeds, settlement agreements contemplating payment of funds, settlement statements issued to the client, documentation relating to sharing litigation costs and attorney fees for subrogated claims, agreements for division of fees between lawyers, guarantees of payment to third

parties out of proceeds recovered on behalf of a client, and copies of bills, receipts or correspondence related to any payments to third parties on behalf of a client (whether made from the client's funds or from the lawyer's funds advanced for the benefit of the client).

APPENDIX D

Sample Chart of Accounts for Law Firms

You will want to adopt a consistent account numbering scheme such as this one:

Account Numbering Scheme:

Cash Accounts begin with number 0

Asset Accounts begin with number 1

Liability Accounts begin with number 2

Equity Accounts begin with number 3

Operating Revenue (income) Accounts begin with number 4

Operating Expense Accounts begin with numbers 5, 6, and 7

Non-operating revenue and expenses, gains and losses accounts begin with 8 or 9

Account Number	Name of Account	Type of Account	Description of Account	To Increase this Account
01	Operating Account	Bank (CASH)	Law firm's business checking or general operating account at bank	Debit
02	Client Trust Account	Bank (CASH)	Law firm's client trust account at bank	Debit
120	Accounts Receivable	Asset	Amounts owed to law firm for services performed but not yet paid for	Debit
130	Advanced Client Costs	Other Current Asset	Costs advanced by law firm for client	Debit
131	Advanced Client Costs: Court Costs	Other Current Asset	Advanced cost: court costs	Debit
132	Advanced Client Costs: Expert Witness Fees	Other Current Asset	Advanced cost: expert witness fees	Debit
133	Advanced Client Costs: Filing Fee	Other Current Asset	Advanced cost: filing fees	Debit
140	Supplies	Asset	Cost of supplies not yet used	Debit
150	Prepaid Insurance	Asset	Cost of insurance paid in advance covering future accounting period	Debit
155	Prepaid Professional Dues	Asset	Cost of professional dues paid in advance covering future accounting period	Debit
160	Land	Fixed Asset	Cost to acquire and prepare land for law firm	Debit
161	Building	Fixed Asset	Cost to acquire and prepare building for law firm	Debit
162	Accumulated Depreciation: Building	Fixed Asset	Amount of building's cost that has been allocated to depreciation expense since the time the building was acquired by law firm	Credit

Account Number	Name of Account	Type of Account	Description of Account	To Increase this Account
170	Equipment	Fixed Asset	Cost of equipment used by law firm	Debit
171	Accumulated Depreciation: Equipment	Fixed Asset	Amount of equipment's cost that has been allocated to depreciation expense since the time the equipment was acquired by law firm	Credit
180	Library	Fixed Asset	Library of law firm, including digital books	Credit
201	Notes Payable	Other Current Liability	The amount of principal due on a loan by law	Credit
210	Accounts Payable	Other Current Liability	The amount owed by law firm to suppliers	Credit
220	Salary Payable	Other Current Liability	Amount owed by law firm to employees for hours worked but not yet paid	Credit
230	Interest Payable	Other Current Liability	Amount of interest on notes payable up until the date of the balance sheet (amount of note × effective interest rate × time period)	Credit
240	Client Trust Liability	Other Current Liability	The Client Trust Account Liability is the total of the subaccounts for each client	Credit
240	Client Trust Liability: Client A	Other Current Liability	Subaccount for Client A's trust account	Credit
250	Mortgage Loan Payable	Other Current Liability	Mortgage loan on law firm building secured by a recorded lien	Credit
310	Attorney's Capital Account	Owner's Equity	Amount lawyer owner has invested in law firm, cash or property, plus any earnings not withdrawn by owner	Credit

Account Number	Name of Account	Type of Account	Description of Account	To Increase this Account
399	Attorney's Draw	Owner's Equity	Amount sole proprietorship owner has withdrawn for personal use during current accounting year; at end of the accounting year, the amount in this account will be transferred into attorney's capital account	Debit
410	Service Revenues or Legal Fee Income	Revenue (Income)	Amount earned by law firm for providing legal services	Credit
420	Reimbursed Client Expense Income	Revenue		
(Income)	Amount repaid by client for costs that had been advanced by law firm	Credit		
500	Salaries Expense	Expense	Expenses incurred for the work performed by salaried employees during the current accounting period	Debit
510	Wages Expense	Expense	Expenses incurred for the work performed by nonsalaried employees paid hourly during the current accounting period	Debit
520	Supplies Expense	Expense	Cost for supplies consumed during the accounting period	Debit
530	Rent Expense	Expense	Cost of occupying rented office during the accounting period	Debit

Account Number	Name of Account	Type of Account	Description of Account	To Increase this Account
540	Utilities Expense	Expense	Cost of utilities used during the accounting period	Debit
545	Telephone Expense	Expense	Cost of telephone service used during the accounting period	Debit
547	Internet Expense	Expense	Cost of Internet service used during the accounting period	Debit
600	Advertising Expense	Expense	Cost for advertising and promotion (other than salaries) incurred by law firm during the accounting period	Debit
610	Website Expense	Expense	Cost of website service used during the accounting period	Debit
700	Library Expense	Expense	Cost of library purchased on subscription incurred by law firm during the accounting period	Debit
710	Research Expense	Expense	Cost for research service incurred by law firm such as West Law or Lexis	Debit
720	CLE Expense	Expense	Cost of continuing legal education expense incurred by law firm during the accounting period	Debit
740	Professional Dues Expense	Expense	Cost for bar association membership expense incurred by law firm during the accounting period	Debit
750	Insurance Expense	Expense	Cost for insurance incurred by law firm during the accounting period	Debit

Account Number	Name of Account	Type of Account	Description of Account	To Increase this Account
770	Depreciation Expense	Expense	Cost of long-term assets allocated to expense during the current account period	Debit
810	Interest Revenue	Revenue (income)	Interest earned on law firm's bank account, investments, or notes payable to law firm	Credit
910	Gain on Sale of Assets	Gain	Gain occurs when the law firm sells one of its assets for more than the asset's book value	Credit
950	Loss on Sale of Assets	Loss	Loss occurs when the law firm sells one of its assets for less than the asset's book value	Debit

APPENDIX E

Sample Client Ledger or Transaction Report

Date	Name	Memo	Ck #	CLIENT COSTS ADVANCED			FEES FOR LEGAL SERVICES			CLIENT TRUST ACCOUNT		
				Costs Advanced	Costs Received	Costs Balance	Fees Charged	Fees Received	AR Balance	Trust Funds Received	Trust Funds Disbursed	Trust Account Balance

APPENDIX F

Sample Reconciliation Statement Form

For Month Ended:			
	CLIENT NAME	CLIENT'S TRUST ACCOUNT BALANCE FROM CLIENT LEDGERS	
	LAW FIRM'S FUNDS FOR BANK CHARGES IF ANY		
Section 1	**TOTAL FROM ALL CLIENT LEDGERS**		
Section 2	**TOTAL FROM TRUST ACCOUNT JOURNAL**		
	BANK STATEMENT		
	Minus Outstanding Checks		
	Plus In Transit Deposits		
Section 3	**RECONCILED BANK STATEMENT BALANCE**		

APPENDIX G

Sample Trust Account Journal or Transaction Register

Date	Deposits To Client Trust Account				Withdrawals from Client Trust Account				Trust Account Balance
	Ck. No.	Receipts Amount	Source	Description of Deposited Item	Ck. No.	Disbursements Amount	Payee	Purpose of Disbursement	Balance

Index